"Masterful! F ... practice and l ... He skillfully ᵥ ... universal func ... , *The Tao of Stress* is a must-read!"

> —**David Wei**, 16th generation lineage holder of Wudang Mountain's Zhang San Feng wellness tradition and founder of Wudang West Cultural Heritage Center

"Bob Santee both expresses the tradition of Taoism accurately in easy-to-understand language and makes this ancient tradition relevant to our modern version of the human dilemma of stress. Readers of this book will learn basic Taoist practices and how to apply them in daily life in order to heal their stress. This is an excellent book for participatory people; mainly those who are willing to be actively involved in their healing. Engaging the Taoist practices as Santee clearly explains them will enable a person to cultivate their natural life energy, thereby not only naturally healing their stress, but also realizing greater health in body, mind, and spirit.

> —**Reggie Pawle, PhD**, cross-cultural psychotherapist and professor of Asian psychologies, at East-West Psychology Service, Kyoto, Japan, and Kansai Gaidai University, Hirakata, Japan

"The words of Robert G. Santee's *The Tao of Stress* are as clear as his obvious command of the philosophy, psychology, and practical application of Taoist principles for calming the 'galloping mind' and simplifying one's life."

> —**Ronald Zelman**, founder of DragonTail Mindfulness, LLC, a company that devotes its energies to helping individuals utilize tai chi, qigong, and Wing Chun kung fu to improve their lives

The
Tao of
Stress

How to Calm, Balance, and Simplify Your Life

Robert G. Santee, PhD

New Harbinger Publications, Inc.

Distributed in Canada by Raincoast Books

Copyright © 2013 by Robert G. Santee
      New Harbinger Publications, Inc.
      5674 Shattuck Avenue
      Oakland, CA 94609
      www.newharbinger.com

Cover design by Amy Shoup
Acquired by Melissa Kirk
Edited by Jasmine Star

Library of Congress Cataloging-in-Publication Data on file

Printed in the United States of America

15   14   13

10   9   8   7   6   5   4   3   2   1

First Printing

Contents

Acknowledgments   v

Introduction   1

Part 1   Understanding Stress and Taoism

1 Stress and Taoism   9

2 Basics of Taoist Meditation   25

Part 2   Simplifying Your Life

3 Simplifying Your Thoughts   41

4 Simplifying Your Behavior   55

5 Not Interfering with Yourself or Others   69

Part 3   Reducing Your Desires

6 Understanding Desires   85

7 Not Getting Entangled in the Activities of the World   99

8 Changing Your Thoughts and Behaviors and Reducing Your
   Desires   113

Part 4 Stilling and Emptying Your Mind

9 The Taoist Body-Based Meditative Core   **129**

10 The Authentic Person   **143**

Moving Forward   **159**

References   **161**

Acknowledgments

I extend deep gratitude to my wife, Charlene; to our son, Ian, and his fiancée, Joy Watanabe; to my son, Aaron, his wife, Karen, and their children, Emma and Lauren; and to my daughter, Jenai, her husband, Jeremy Kubo, and their children, Liliana, Cameron, Kalani, and Payson. I thank them for being who they are and being an intimate part of my journey through life, for their humor and support, and for creating a peaceful environment that allowed me to write this book.

I extend appreciation to Marie Burghardt, my fellow traveler in the worlds of martial arts, qigong, teaching, Taoism, and assessment, and a great friend for over thirty years, for being who she is, and for her support, humor, insight, and therapeutic intuition.

I also send appreciation to Ronald Zelman, another fellow traveler in the world of martial arts, qigong, and teaching, the master of the dragon-tail, and a great friend for over thirty years, for being who he is, and for his support, humor, and insight, and for the fascinating existential discussions we've shared.

I thank my weekly wise elders in my taijiquan and qigong group—Madeline Wong, Edith Watanabe, Herb Hamada, and Jan Martin—for their friendship, smiles, laughter, support, and great energy as we practice these wonderful arts.

I thank Xiu Zhang, my baguazhang and qigong laoshi, for teaching me these arts and for the wonderful philosophical and cultural conversations we had about them; for her insights, humor, and friendship; and for introducing me to and arranging my training in taijiquan, baguazhang, and qigong in Beijing.

I acknowledge Zhijian Cai, my taijiquan and qigong shifu, for his insights and for teaching me the standardized taijiquan forms, as well as weapons, push hands, the Yijinjing, and sitting and standing meditation.

I thank New Harbinger Publications for making this book possible. Special thanks go to Wendy Millstine, who took the first step by asking me if I wanted to write a book and then guiding, reviewing, and editing my proposal, and to Melissa Kirk, Jess Beebe, Nicola Skidmore, and Angela Autry Gorden for guiding me through the process and reviewing the chapters as I wrote. I also want to thank Jasmine Star for her extensive review and copyediting of the manuscript.

My thanks also go to my assistant, Jan Martin, and my secretary, Pam Silva-Patrinos, both at Chaminade University, for their humor, assistance, and help.

Introduction

In a symposium on Taoism at the American Psychological Association's annual convention in Washington, DC, in August 2011, which was probably the APA's first such symposium, Donald Davis, PhD, Reggie Pawle, PhD, Stephen Jackowicz, PhD, and I conducted a panel session entitled *Building Bridges between Daoism and Psychology: Integrating Mind, Body and Spirit to Enhance Psychological Outcomes.* My presentation was *Daoism and Counseling: An Integrative Approach for Adapting to the Environment.* The symposium was well attended and well received.

Wendy Millstine, an acquisitions editor for New Harbinger Publications, attended the symposium, and afterward she asked if any of the panel members would like to write a self-help book from a Taoist perspective. I said yes. That was my first step, and this book is the result.

What This Book Is About

In the 2011 *Stress in America* survey, conducted by the American Psychological Association (APA 2012), 39 percent of the 1,226 adults surveyed reported that their stress levels had increased from the previous year, whereas only 17 percent indicated it had decreased. A recent survey (Regus 2012) of more than 16,000 adult workers in fourteen countries asked people about their stress on the job. An average of 48 percent indicated that their stress levels had increased from the previous year, with 47 percent of workers in the United States indicating that their stress levels on the job had increased from the previous year.

This book is about the problem of stress, specifically chronic stress, and what you can do to reduce, eliminate, and prevent it. It is explicitly about the application of Taoist teachings and principles to the problem of chronic stress. Taoism, a 2,500-year-old philosophy, religion, and psychology, is a way of life that is focused on being in harmony with the continually changing world around us.

In this book, the focus is on a way of life that eliminates chronic stress so that we can be in harmony with the world around us and all of its life-forms. The specific Taoist path for eliminating chronic stress discussed here is found scattered throughout Taoist writings. However, it's best described in the appendix of the eighth-century text the *Zuowanglun* (*Discussions on Sitting in Oblivion or Forgetfulness*). The path consists of three interrelated and integrated components: simplifying life, reducing desires, and stilling and emptying the mind.

Taoism often makes extensive use of stories to convey its essential teachings, and I have followed that practice in this book. Likewise, I've followed the Taoist principle of utilizing repetition as a teaching device. While these approaches do not necessarily align with a typical Western approach, they are part of the Taoist tradition—a tradition that excels in helping people overcome chronic stress.

The Structure of This Book

Aside from the introduction and conclusion, this book is divided into four parts. The two chapters in part 1 cover some of the basics of stress and Taoism. The remaining three parts are based on the three components of the *Zuowanglun*. Part 2, "Simplifying Your Life," has chapters on simplifying your thoughts, simplifying your behavior, and not interfering with yourself or others. Part 3, "Reducing Your Desires," has chapters on understanding desires, not getting entangled in the activities of the world, and changing your thoughts and behaviors and reducing your desires. Part 4, "Stilling and Emptying Your Mind," has chapters on the Taoist body-based meditative core and Taoism's concept of the authentic person.

Starting with chapter 2, each chapter consists of two parts: the mental approach to addressing chronic stress, followed by the physical approach, primarily in the form of qigong postures. For the purposes of this book, the mental and physical approaches have equal weight. You need to do both.

The Mental and Physical Approaches

In the mental approach, I'll guide you in consciously, intentionally, and directly bringing a specific problem into awareness, examining and reflecting upon its cause, generating a solution for resolving it, and then implementing the solution. Each chapter focuses on a specific context, the problems within that context that give rise to chronic stress, how it is maintained, and how it can be eliminated. The mental approach can be viewed as being both reactive ("I am chronically stressed and I want to eliminate it") and proactive ("Having gotten rid of it, I don't want it to return").

The physical approach is more general in nature and doesn't intentionally or directly focus on any specific problem or its cause, other than the obvious concern with chronic stress: your health and well-being. It focuses on teaching you proper body alignment and how to root and center yourself by training your attention, concentration, and breathing. It also includes instruction in how to stretch and relax your body. A rooted and centered body is healthy and not chronically stressed. This approach is based on the observation that by calming and relaxing the body, the mind will relax and become still and empty. This will help ease your chronic stress.

Another benefit of the physical approach is that the more you practice it, the less time you'll spend engaging in and reinforcing the problematic thinking, desires, and behaviors that lead to ongoing physical and psychological agitation and create chronic stress. Thus, the physical approach addresses the same areas that the mental approach does, but in an entirely different manner.

Because this Taoist path incorporates both a mental approach and a physical approach, and because it addresses mind, body, and environment, it is holistic in nature. To remedy chronic stress, you need to incorporate both approaches into your life.

Qigong

Qigong literally means developing, working with, and cultivating qi. *Qi* is both vital energy and breath. When a person is ill, her qi isn't circulating freely throughout her body. Her mind, body, and environment aren't in harmony. She has lost her center and root. The practice of qigong is focused on finding and maintaining your center and root; allowing your qi to circulate freely; reestablishing and maintaining the harmony between your mind, body, and environment; teaching you to relax; and helping you reduce or eliminate chronic stress.

There is considerable research validating the benefits of qigong and *taijiquan* (often spelled tai chi or tai chi chuan). The research covers both physical and psychological problems associated with lifestyle and chronic stress (for example, Wayne 2003; Jahnke et al. 2010; Rogers, Larkey, and Keller 2009). There is also considerable research validating the physical and psychological benefits of meditation (Davis and Hayes 2011; Walsh and Shapiro 2006).

I'll teach two basic types of qigong in this book. Both are extremely old. The first is the Sitting Eight Pieces of Brocade (Baduanjin), which incorporates both still and moving postures. I will teach all eight Baduanjin postures in this book. The second is the Method of Changing and Transforming the Muscles and Tendons (Yijinjing). This is a standing form that incorporates both still and moving postures. You will learn eight postures from this form.

Starting with chapter 2, each chapter will include instruction in one Baduanjin posture and one Yijinjing posture. In each subsequent chapter, I'll instruct you in the next posture in the two sequences. After learning each new posture, make sure you link it to the previous postures. For example, after learning and practicing the third Baduanjin posture, go back and perform the first posture, followed by the second posture and then the third. Use this process for all the postures. Baduanjin and Yijinjing were developed to have practitioners do the postures sequentially, one right after another, until all are completed. By practicing in this way, you'll receive optimal benefits from your practice.

Eating, Drinking, Sleeping, Exercise, and Chronic Stress

Chapters 4, 5, and 6 all discuss eating, drinking, sleeping, exercise, and chronic stress, doing so in the contexts of behavior, noninterference, and desires, respectively. Each context looks at eating, drinking, sleeping, and exercise from a slightly different perspective. Although each of these contexts is explored in a separate chapter, in Taoism, everything is interrelated, and thus these contexts overlap and are integrated with each other.

Chinese Texts

The ancient Taoist texts I referred to are the *Daodejing* (sometimes spelled *Tao Te Ching*, and often translated as *The Way and Its Power*), the *Zhuangzi* (no translation, as it is a man's name), the *Liezi* (no translation, as it is a man's name), the *Zuowanglun* (*Discussions on Sitting in Oblivion or Forgetfulness*), the *Neiye* (*Inner Explorations*), the *Yijing* (sometimes spelled *I Ching*, and often translated as *The Book of Changes*), the *Neijing* (*Classic of Internal Medicine*), and the *Bingfa* (*The Art of War*). Several of these are over 2,200 years old: the *Yijing*, traditionally believed to have developed over time and attributed to numerous authors; the *Daodejing*, traditionally attributed to philosopher Laozi (sixth to fifth century BCE); the *Zhuangzi*, written in part by philosopher Zhuangzi (370–290 BCE); the *Neiye* (fourth century BCE), which is a chapter in the *Guanzi* (compiled in the first century BCE and representing anonymous essays from the fifth through first centuries BCE); and the *Bingfa*, traditionally believed to have been written by Sunzi (sometimes spelled Sun Tzu; sixth century BCE), a general. The *Neijing*, of unknown authorship, is approximately 2,000 years old. The *Liezi*, traditionally attributed to philosopher Liezi, is believed to be about 1,700 years old. The *Zuowanglun*, written by Taoist master Sima Chengzhen (647–735 CE), is approximately 1,300 years old. For the specific selections I refer to in this book, I've referenced my own translations from the original Chinese.

Keeping a Journal

Throughout this book, after you do various activities, practices, and the qigong, I'll ask you to record your experiences in a journal. You can do this in whatever format works for you: in a notebook, on a computer, and so on. Keeping this journal will allow you to reflect on your experiences and give you a record of your challenges and progress as you journey on the Taoist path for the removal of chronic stress. The act of journaling itself is commonly thought to be a useful therapeutic tool and a helpful way to reduce chronic stress (Howes 2011).

How to Use This Book

This book is structured to be followed sequentially, in both the mental approach and the physical approach. As noted previously, it's important to incorporate and integrate both approaches and treat them as being of equal weight. There is no rush to get through the book. Take your time, especially with the qigong.

Now it's time to start your journey. As Laozi said in chapter 64 of the *Daodejing* (Wang 1993, 249), "A journey of 1,000 miles begins with your first step."

Part 1

Understanding Stress and Taoism

Chapter 1

Stress and Taoism

This chapter consists of two parts. The first part explores the basics of stress, the fight-or-flight response, and the problems associated with chronic stress. The second part provides an introduction to Taoism and explains its solution to the problem of chronic stress.

Normal Stress

At the most basic level, stress is the changes that happen in the body and brain to help us face challenges and solve problems in our ever-changing world. These changes primarily consist of increased energy, acute focus of attention and concentration, motivation to act, and actually acting. This is normal stress.

Normal stress serves to help us find a solution to a problem. For example, after waking up in the morning and while still lying in bed, you probably experience a sensation that indicates you need to go to the bathroom. This is the problem. You need to sit up, then stand up, and then walk to the bathroom. This is the solution. To achieve this, the body and brain need to go through a series of changes.

You need to remain focused on going to the bathroom. You need to be motivated to get up and go to the bathroom. You need to increase your energy levels so you can remain focused and motivated and actually get up and go to the bathroom. The changes in position from lying in bed, to sitting, to standing, and then to walking require that you expend more energy than needed to simply lie in bed. Thus, your heart rate and blood pressure increase, and your breathing speeds up to deliver energy to your muscles so you can make it to the bathroom. This is an example of the normal and natural type of stress that the body and brain experience every day.

The Fight-or-Flight Response

When normal stress is threat based, we call it the fight-or-flight response or stress response. The fight-or-flight response evolved to help us face infrequent immediate threats and solve them quickly, with the response shutting down after the threat has passed. It differs from normal stress in that it is threat based, the changes that occur are generally much more intense, and it just happens unconsciously, without thinking about it.

The primary function of the fight-or-flight response is to help resolve the perceived potential threat by increasing the body's energy production and sending the energy to various physiological systems that put us on alert, motivate us to act, and prepare us to fight, flee, or freeze in case we actually have to fight, flee, or freeze. We are wired this way for our own protection and survival.

Here's an example of how the fight-or-flight response leads to a solution to the problem posed by a threat. Let's say it's late at night and you're walking alone to your car in a dimly lit parking lot. You feel anxious and tense. Your sole focus is on getting to your car safely. You reach your car, open the door, check the backseat to make sure no one is there, and then get in. You lock the doors, start your car, and drive away. As you start to drive away, you can feel your body begin to relax.

What happened here? You perceived a threat. You wanted to get to your car safely and drive home. Your fight-or-flight response was activated automatically and appropriately because you're wired this way. You were alone and you perceived a genuine potential physical threat to your life: the setting and everything associated with it. The tension, anxiety, threat-based thinking, and single focus are all parts of the fight-or-flight response, alerting you to danger and preparing you to face a potential threat. Once you resolved the threat by safely reaching your car and driving away, your fight-or-flight response automatically turned off.

There are two basic reasons why the fight-or-flight response automatically turns off once a threat is resolved. The first is that, when we are triggered, the bodily systems associated with the stress response are pushed beyond their normal limits, and they can't sustain this sort of intensity in the long term without being harmed. The second reason is that energy is diverted away from certain body systems that don't participate during the stress response, such as digestion, and when those systems don't get enough energy to function, they may also be damaged or deteriorate.

Chronic Stress

Stress becomes a problem when the fight-or-flight response isn't turned off or is too easily activated. Chronic stress is the ongoing activation of the fight-or-flight response that can result from continual perception of potential threats or the frequent activation of the fight-or-flight response due to everyday hassles that are perceived as threats. When this happens, the fight-or-flight response isn't functioning properly. It isn't helping us as it's supposed to. In fact, it is harming us.

The results of the American Psychological Association's *Stress in America* surveys (APA 2007, 2008, 2009, 2010, 2012) clearly demonstrate that chronic stress has significant harmful effects on physical, psychological, interpersonal, and occupational health. Based on the results across the five surveys, the most recent *Stress in America* survey suggests that "the nation is on the verge of a stress-induced public health crisis" (APA 2012, 5). Research indicates that 60 to 90 percent of symptoms reported to medical doctors by patients during office visits are associated with, worsened by, or caused by chronic stress (Benson 1998; WebMD 2011). Chronic stress is clearly not good for us.

Here's an example of how this manifests. Let's say that as you're leaving work for the day, your boss comes over and asks you to do a twenty-minute presentation first thing the next morning at an office meeting of about thirty fellow employees. She wants you to talk about an idea you mentioned to her the previous day. Your mouth immediately gets dry. Your stomach feels queasy. You hesitantly agree.

On the way home, you can only think about the presentation and all the things that that could possibly go wrong. You get home and try to eat some dinner, but your stomach still feels queasy and your mouth is dry, so you don't eat much. You then spend the rest of the evening planning your presentation. You have a hard time staying focused because your worry keeps getting in the way. You go to bed and have a difficult time getting to sleep. Once you finally fall asleep, you keep waking up.

You don't feel rested when you wake up the next morning. You try to eat something, but you don't feel hungry. As you drive to work, all you can think about is your presentation and what could go wrong with it. You arrive at work and head to the meeting room.

Your heart rate is speeding. Your breathing is rapid and shallow. Your stomach is still queasy, and your mouth is really dry. You're sweating considerably even though the room is quite cool. Your muscles are tense and achy. You can't stop worrying about the presentation being a disaster.

Your boss introduces you. You walk up to the podium and look out at the audience. There are a lot of people. You look down at your notes. You try to speak, but nothing comes out. You simply freeze.

In this case, your fight-or-flight response has been continuously activated for hours on end. It was inappropriately activated because no genuine threat existed, and worse, it provided no assistance in addressing the perceived threat: your fear of looking like a fool in front of your fellow workers. In fact, activation of the fight-or-flight response was detrimental because it made the situation worse, and because its chronic activation negatively impacted your sleep, eating, thinking, and overall physical and psychological well-being. It was never deactivated because you kept thinking about the perceived threat and worrying, and as a result, the problem wasn't resolved.

Unfortunately, we are wired to look for threats, and the brain doesn't make distinctions between physical threats, psychosocial threats, potential threats, anticipated threats, self-generated threats, and imagined threats. All of these can turn on and maintain the fight-or-flight response. Anything that we perceive as threatening, no matter how minor, has the potential to activate and maintain the fight-or-flight response, whether that threat involves how we think we should behave, how we think others should behave, or how we think the world should work. No matter what their form, perceived threats are seen as potentially endangering our existence at some level, be it physical, psychological, or social.

Physical and Psychological Effects of Normal Stress

How we physically and psychologically respond to perceived threats, real or imagined, depends on the stressor's context. Our responses are also associated with our genetic makeup, our family history, our life experiences, how we construct our world, and our coping mechanisms.

Once the fight-or-flight response is turned on, a number of physical and psychological changes immediately occur. Physically, heart rate increases, blood pressure goes up, breathing becomes rapid and shallow, muscles tense, blood forms clots more quickly, fats are broken down and released into the bloodstream, blood flow is rerouted from the body's surface and extremities to muscles, sweating increases, insulin production decreases, digestion is inhibited, parts of the immune system shut down (Segerstrom and Miller 2004), and the hormones adrenaline, norepinephrine, and cortisol are released into the bloodstream.

All of these changes occur for several purposes: increasing energy; transporting energy to areas in the body that need it so we can fight, flee, or freeze; not wasting energy on parts of the body that aren't necessary for fighting, fleeing, or freezing; and protecting the body from the perceived threat. Once the threat is resolved, the fight-or-flight response ceases and bodily systems return to normal functioning.

The primary psychological changes that happen as a result of the perception of a potential threat are all related to keeping us aware of and responding to the threat. Regarding survival, we cannot afford to be distracted. In most cases, we initially feel tense and on edge. These feelings alert us to potential dangers. Our attention continually scans the environment looking for potential threats. This hyperarousal keeps us apprehensive, concerned, and worrying about potential threats in the environment. Our concentration focuses on anything our attention isolates as a potential threat and then keeps us directed toward it.

Threat-based thinking has certain qualities: it is self-centered, biased, absolute, black-and-white, judgmental, inflexible, not distractible, and mechanical. For our distant ancestors, any deviation or distraction from the single focus of the threat might have resulted in death. Our hypervigilance, hyperarousal, and threat-based thinking work together to alert us to potential threats, keep us focused upon them, and motivate us to face them. Once a perceived threat is resolved, our attention, concentration, arousal, emotions, and ways of thinking return to normal.

Physical and Psychological Effects of Chronic Stress

When the fight-or-flight response is chronically or frequently activated, the physical and psychological changes that occur are detrimental to our health. The human body can't withstand the intense changes of the stress response on a continuous or long-term basis. Just imagine what could occur if the intense changes of a normal stress response weren't allowed to return to normal. Physically, the heart would be overworked, hypertension would result from continual high blood pressure, breathing would be compromised, energy production would hindered, problems with digestion could occur, ongoing high blood sugar levels could lead to diabetes, and rapid clotting of blood could lead to a stroke or heart attack.

Continual muscular tension could lead to headaches, vision problems, breathing problems, mobility issues, problems with posture, and generally feeling tired, sore, and stiff. The immune system is suppressed, which makes us more susceptible to bacterial and viral infections and compromises our overall resistance and healing capabilities (Segerstrom and Miller 2004).

Continually elevated levels of stress hormones are also detrimental to our health and well-being. In addition, they perpetuate the cycle by keeping the fight-or-flight response activated and on high alert. Chronic high levels of cortisol suppress the immune system and compromise the function of insulin, resulting in elevated blood sugar levels, increases in appetite, and cravings for high-fat foods. High cortisol levels also lead to fat being stored in the abdominal area (Bouchez 2011), decreased bone density, and atrophy of muscles (Scott 2011; McEwen 2002).

In terms of the psychological impacts of chronic stress, the mind is continually agitated and the ability to concentrate and think is compromised. Negative thinking dominates our worldview. Whining, complaining, moaning, criticizing, demeaning, sarcasm, mockery, derision, scorning, disdain, ridicule, contempt, and so on are all forms of negative thinking, and negative thinking is always threat based. This perpetuates the cycle, as threat-based thinking activates and maintains the fight-or-flight response, preventing us from being able to see potential solutions to the problem.

In addition to all the obvious forms of negative (threat-based) thinking listed above, any type of ongoing absolute, restrictive, inflexible, judgmental, black-and-white, or either-or thinking (live or die, good or evil, and so on) can inappropriately activate the fight-or-flight response. This happens because any thoughts or opinions contrary to this absolute, black-and-white perspective may be perceived as a threat to how we structure and relate to the world.

Finally, ongoing anxiety is clearly a problem, as it involves inappropriately labeling neutral or nonthreatening stimuli as potentially threatening. With ongoing anxiety, we are constantly apprehensive, worrying, and obsessive. Attention and concentration are fragmented, and the mind bounces around looking for potential threats.

Psychosocial Threats

The list of potential perceived threats is endless. You can simply be sitting in a chair at home and start worrying about the economy, global warming, your job, money, family issues, friends, politics, arguments you had or may have, unrealistic deadlines and goals, whether or not your daughter's wedding in six months will go off without any problems, and on and on. Whatever its focus, this worrying will set off your fight-or-flight response and cause you to be stressed. If your worrying becomes excessive and ongoing, the fight-or-flight response is continually activated and you become chronically stressed.

Another source of potential stress is the complexity of life. The more things you think you need to address, however small and essentially irrelevant they may be, the more likely you are to perceive potential threats, activating your fight-or-flight response. Many people try to deal with long to-do lists by multitasking. However, attempting to do a number of things at the same time can compromise the ability to attend, focus, and concentrate (Rosen 2008). This can drain a person's energy and result in stress.

Things that we desire and don't have, whether tangible or intangible, are also potential threats, as we associate them with our self-worth. We wonder what our family, friends, and society will think of us if we don't have these things. As long as we allow our self-worth to be determined by others and continue to wish for these things, we may feel threatened and remain chronically stressed.

The same is true of things we desired and now have, whether tangible or intangible, in this case because of the anxiety and fear about possibly losing them. The threat of potential loss activates the stress response, and as long as we harbor the fear of losing these things, our fight-or-flight response will remain activated.

Practice   Examining Your Stress

I'd like you to try something that may make the preceding discussion of stress much more directly relevant to you and your concerns. This exercise is about your experience with stress. It consists of two parts: examining an appropriate activation of the fight-or-flight response in your own life, and examining an inappropriate activation of the fight-or-flight response in your own life. You can use your journal to answer the questions in this exercise; that way you'll have plenty of space to write your responses.

First, think of a situation in your life when the fight-or-flight response was activated appropriately—in a way that helped you address the perceived threat.

1. Write down what happened. What was the problem or threat that activated your fight-or-flight response?

2. Think about what you noticed happening in your mind and body as you faced the problem or threat. Do you remember if your heart was pounding or you were breathing faster, sweating, or feeling anxious or tense? Do you remember what you were thinking about? Did you stay focused on the problem or threat? Were you able to make a connection in that moment between the changes that you noticed and the problem or threat?

3. Write down everything you remember about how these physical and psychological changes helped you face the threat or solve the problem.

4. Do you remember what happened after the problem or threat was resolved? Did you feel more relaxed? Did the changes you experienced as you faced the problem or threat go away after it was resolved? Did you notice a difference between how you felt, physically and psychologically, when you were facing the problem or threat and how you felt after it was resolved?

Now think about an instance when your fight-or-flight response was activated inappropriately—in a way that didn't help you address the perceived problem or threat.

1. Write down what happened and what you noticed in your body and mind. What was the problem or threat that activated your fight-or-flight response?

2. Note whether these changes and the inappropriate activation of your fight-or-flight response helped you address the problem or threat or whether they interfered with resolving it.

3. Did you notice your voice becoming louder or higher, inflaming an interpersonal conflict? Did your thoughts race and make it difficult to concentrate? Were you so distracted that you forgot something important?

4. Did inappropriate activation of the fight-or-flight response make your situation worse in any way? For example, did worrying about the problem or threat make it difficult for you to get to sleep or stay asleep?

How Taoism Can Help with Stress

At this point, you may be thinking that chronic stress is a modern problem, and wondering how the ancient philosophy of Taoism could be helpful in addressing it. However, chronic stress and its impacts on physical and psychological health were recognized and seen as problematic by ancient Taoist practitioners and authors at least 2,500 years ago, and Taoism has provided an avenue for addressing these problems for just as long.

Chronic Stress from a Taoist Perspective

In Taoism, chronic stress is seen as being out of harmony with the inevitable and continual process of change and transformation. When we are out of harmony, we have lost our center and root, and this has several implications:

- Our energy or breath doesn't freely circulate throughout the body and may be blocked or restricted in various parts of the body.

- Our thoughts, desires, emotions, behavior, lifestyle, environment, or some combination of these are excessive or deficient.

- We are fragmented because mind and body are continually agitated.

- Our mind, body, and environment aren't integrated.

- Our life is too complex.

Most Westerners have a different view of chronic stress, seeing it as having a continuously or frequently activated fight-or-flight response, being unable to cope with environmental demands, and so on. However, in both points of view, the physical and psychological symptoms and the underlying causes are the same. For both, habitual threat-based thinking and behaviors, along with threat-based desires, are the primary sources of chronic stress. Given that both approaches recognize the same sorts of physical and psychological symptoms and root causes, Taoist teachings, practices, and techniques are definitely relevant to easing or eliminating chronic stress.

Basic Concepts of Taoism

The various traditions, sects, teachings, texts, and practices that exist within Taoism are gathered under this label because they have a number of commonalities. These commonalities are the basic concepts that comprise the foundation of Taoism. They are also directly relevant to defining and easing chronic stress.

Yin and Yang

In Taoism, existence is seen as a continual, cyclic process of change and transformation. The harmonious interrelationship between the complementary cosmic forces of *yin and yang* provides the most basic explanation of this continual, cyclic process of change and transformation. Everything, including our physical and psychological aspects, consists of various mixtures or patterns of yin and yang. Every thought, emotion, action, behavior, change, and transformation is due to the influence of and relationship between the cosmic forces of yin and yang.

Depending on the context, in some cases yang is more dominant, while in others yin is more dominant. In some contexts, there is a balance between yin and yang. Some examples of this harmonious, complementary interrelationship of yin and yang are earth/sky, contraction/expansion, inhalation/exhalation, night/day, passive/active, sad/happy, off/on, and stillness/movement.

Probably the easiest way to think about yin and yang is to consider the process of reproduction. The female (yin) unites with the male (yang), and in the process of sharing, an offspring is created (transformation), which consists of contributions of both the mother (yin) and the father (yang). If the offspring is male, yang characteristics are dominant. If female, yin characteristics are dominant. In both cases, however, the other, complementary component is present and influential. The offspring then develops (changes) and eventually participates in the reproductive cycle.

When our thoughts, desires, emotions, lifestyle, environment, or behaviors are excessive (characterized by too much yin or yang) or deficient (characterized by insufficient yin or yang), we lose our root and are inflexible, not centered, and out of harmony—in other words, chronically stressed. The goal of Taoism in regard to the removal of chronic stress is to reestablish a harmonious relationship between yin and yang—one that's neither excessive nor deficient—so that we become rooted and centered.

Qi

As mentioned, qi is both vital energy and breath. It circulates throughout the universe and throughout the body. It is the basic building block of all things—organic and inorganic. It takes on the various shapes and configurations that make up our world through the workings of yin and yang. We receive our original qi from our parents and maintain our lives through the qi we receive from breathing, eating, and drinking.

When the circulation of our qi is excessive or deficient and therefore compromised due to our thoughts, desires, emotions, behaviors, lifestyle, or environment, we lose our center, are no longer rooted, and become inflexible. Yin and yang are not in harmony. Mind, body, and environment are not integrated. We are chronically stressed.

The various Taoist practices, techniques, and meditations that you'll learn throughout this book are all oriented toward restoring a free flow of qi throughout the body. As a result, you will become centered, rooted, and flexible. Mind, body, and environment will be integrated. Yin and yang will be in harmony. You will be free from chronic stress.

Tao

When Taoists talk about being in harmony, ultimately they're referring to being in harmony with Tao. *Tao* is the creative source of everything, including nature and its rhythmic patterns. Tao is essentially the continually changing, interrelated, harmonious, interactive process of freely circulating qi being shaped, changed, and transformed by yin and yang.

Tao is often described as the great passageway—a dynamic empty space through which everything comes into being, transforms, and then returns. As dynamic empty space, Tao allows all things to function and doesn't interfere with or get entangled in the continual process of change and transformation.

When we interfere with the natural, cyclic process of change and transformation through our thoughts, desires, emotions, behaviors, and lifestyle, we fragment mind, body, and environment. We make our world complex, absolute, and inflexible. We are out of balance. As a result, we aren't centered, rooted, or flexible. We are chronically stressed. We aren't in harmony with Tao.

Tian

Depending on the context, *tian* is often translated as "nature," "sky," or "heaven." Tian is a manifestation of Tao. It is the creative, interrelated, rhythmic pattern of the continual process of change and transformation expressed through the various configurations of qi manifested by yin and yang. For Taoists, nature is a role model for our behavior. When we don't follow the patterns of nature, we become fragmented and, eventually, chronically stressed.

Ziran

Ziran, or naturalness, is being in harmony with the continual process of change and transformation that we call nature. Ziran essentially means not interfering with ourselves, not interfering with others, and not getting entangled in the affairs of the world. Our thoughts, desires, emotions, behaviors, and lifestyle are neither excessive nor deficient. Qi circulates freely throughout the body. Life isn't complex. We are flexible and able to adapt. We aren't chronically stressed.

The Taoist Path

Across all types of Taoism, the Taoist path for removing chronic stress and becoming harmonious with Tao is threefold: simplifying life, reducing desires, and stilling and emptying the mind. All three components of this interrelated Taoist path focus on removing complex, inflexible, excessive, and deficient thoughts, desires, emotions, behaviors, and lifestyles that create the continual agitation in both body and mind that leads to chronic stress.

Basic Taoist Techniques

All of the various Taoist meditative techniques and practices are grounded in five key components:

- Posture

- Attention

- Concentration

- Natural breathing

- Nonjudgmental, flexibly focused, unbiased, detached observation of what is happening to you and around you in the present

This last component is a type of awareness known as *guan*. You may be more familiar with a similar concept in Buddhism, called mindfulness. All five components are basic to simplifying life, reducing desires, and stilling and emptying the mind. They are fundamental to stopping the continual agitation of both mind and body. I'll discuss them in greater detail in chapter 2.

Taoist meditative techniques and practices are essentially of two types: sitting and standing. Both the sitting and standing techniques can be either still or moving. In some cases, a technique incorporates both. Some of the more common practices are qigong and taijiquan. In appearance, qigong is a lot like various types of stretching exercises. If you aren't familiar with taijiquan, it looks like a very slow-moving form of self-defense that's relaxed, soft, and quiet. It doesn't show any strength or power in its movements, hand strikes, and kicks.

Taoism's behavioral practices are also grounded in five key components:

- Not interfering with ourselves

- Not trying to coerce or force others to do something for our benefit

- Creating a situation that is conducive to our growth and that of others

- Not being controlled by or getting entangled with the affairs of the world

- Being flexible

Conclusion

This chapter laid a foundation for understanding the fight-or-flight response, chronic stress, and a Taoist approach to managing stress. The next chapter will explore the basics of Taoist mediation. You will also learn some Taoist meditation techniques. I believe that these techniques and the others you'll learn throughout this book will be immensely helpful to you as you journey along the path toward freedom from chronic stress.

Chapter 2

Basics of Taoist Meditation

As noted in the previous chapter, Taoists see chronic stress as being due to a continually agitated mind and body. Taoist meditation is a fundamental strategy for stopping this continual agitation of mind and body. Throughout this book, I will weave together Taoist mediation with the three components of the Taoist path: simplifying life, reducing desires, and stilling and emptying the mind.

Five Components of Meditation

Taoist meditation, whatever the form, consists of the five basic components mentioned in chapter 1: posture, attention, concentration, breathing, and guan, or nonjudgmental, unbiased, detached observation of the present moment. In the following sections, I'll discuss each of these components individually and how they relate to each other. It is important to note, however, that these five components essentially compose one interrelated process.

Posture

Correct posture or alignment is fundamental to all Taoist practices, including meditation. Whether we are sitting, standing, or moving, if our bodies aren't in the proper posture or alignment, we won't be rooted and centered. If we aren't rooted and centered, our mind, breath, muscles, tendons, ligaments, bones, organs, nerves, and so on will be strained and stressed because they aren't functioning in a natural manner.

Exercise   Awareness of Posture

Try the following experiment for a direct experience of the difference between proper and improper alignment: Stand hunched slightly forward, with your shoulders pulled up, your jaw pulled down toward your chest, and your eyes looking downward. You should immediately notice the stress and strain on your neck, chest, spine, knees, and various muscles. This position also puts undue stress on your organs. You will probably have a sense of being off balance because your body is pulled forward. Your breathing may feel compromised. As a result of all this unpleasantness and stress, your mind may be agitated, making you feel tense. This improper and excessive position is harmful to both your mind and your body.

Next, stand up straight, with your eyes looking forward, and visualize that the middle of the top of your head is gently being pulled up, as though you're suspended from above like a puppet on a string. You should notice that you feel as if your head is being pulled back slightly; that your jaw is parallel to the ground, rather than being tilted up or down; your shoulders drop naturally; your spine is both pulled up and sinks as it finds its proper natural alignment; and your feet feel as if they're sinking or rooting through the ground. You should have a clear sense of being centered and relaxed. Your mind will probably feel focused, still, and empty. Your breathing will be more natural. You may even get a sense of warmth flowing through your body, or a pulsating or tingling sensation as your qi starts to flow freely. Note what you feel and discover, and record this in your journal.

The difference in feeling between these two positions is quite clear. The first is stressful and harmful, whereas the second is relaxing and beneficial. You may want to check your posture periodically throughout the day and note what you discover. Once again, record your feelings and discoveries in your journal. The journal record will give you a baseline to track your progress.

Attention

Distractibility, or poor attention, is clearly a problem in our society today, as we are bombarded with an endless variety of distractions: the Internet, cell phones, cable TV, computers, video games, smartphones, tablets, and on and on. This explosion in information technology, which has conditioned us to expect instantaneous responses to our inquiries, has resulted in a high degree of intolerance and irritation if we don't immediately get what we want (Ratey 2008). Because of this conditioning, if we don't receive immediate feedback, we often quickly lose interest in the original object of attraction and are easily bored. Our attention darts from object to object, looking for something novel or of greater intensity to hold it.

The common habit of channel surfing is a clear example of being impatient and easily distractible. This also tends to happen as we browse the Internet, clicking from link to link. As our attention races all over the place, our thoughts become increasingly agitated as they bounce from one object to another.

However, the problem of being easily distracted and unable to maintain attention isn't a new condition. It's discussed throughout Taoist literature from the last 2,300 years. Human attention doesn't wish to sit still. As a result, our minds are continually agitated as our thoughts race wildly. An agitated and racing mind is a clear indicator that we aren't relaxed. In fact, it tells us that we are chronically stressed. Within Taoist literature, this continually agitated and racing mind is often referred to as "galloping while sitting."

To stop the racing of the mind and gain control of attention, Taoist practices focus on interacting with the world and ourselves from the abdomen or a position of being centered. For Taoists, the abdomen is the location of the lower *dantian*, located two to three inches below the belly button. The lower dantian is not only the center of the body, but also the center of our gravity, balance, and energy. Unlike the situation with the senses and the mind, there is no object of distraction for the lower dantian. Learning how to focus upon and develop this center is fundamental for the practice of Taoist meditation and eliminating chronic stress, as doing so allows us to still and quiet the mind.

Jack's Story

Jack, who was fifteen years old, had developed a habit of slouching whether he was walking or sitting. In addition to putting undue stress on his spine, neck, chest, and various muscles, his posture appeared to reflect a depressed attitude. When anybody pointed this out to him, it was usually in a negative manner ("Hey, hunchback!"), making him feel physically and psychologically worse.

One day his favorite uncle, Kent, who practiced qigong regularly, came to visit. In a very caring way, Kent walked over to greet Jack, who was standing off by himself. He put one hand on Jack's shoulder and gently slid his other hand down to the middle of Jack's lower back and softly pushed in. Jack felt his shoulders go back, his chest go forward, and his head go up. The normal heaviness he felt sank to the ground.

Kent, with a big smile on his face, asked Jack how he felt. Jack, who was also smiling, said he felt really good. Kent explained to Jack how important good posture is for both physical and psychological health and told him that this was one of the things he had learned from his qigong practice.

Concentration

Because Taoism recognizes the problem of distractibility, it includes practices for developing, cultivating, and sustaining attention. Sustained attention is concentration. Taoist meditative practices often develop concentration by having practitioners focus their attention on the lower dantian and maintain it there, without dwelling on anything else.

When the mind drifts (and it will) as you practice the various forms of Taoist meditation, simply ignore the thoughts that arise. Don't dwell upon or think about them, whatever they may be. Don't make judgments about how poorly you're doing. Just acknowledge that you've been distracted and return to your focal point. If you don't dwell upon or judge thoughts when they arise, they will naturally be extinguished. For thoughts and judgments to remain, we must continually dwell upon or feed them. If they are to be sustained, we must give them energy. When we stop providing them with energy, they simply pass from consciousness. As you consistently and regularly practice this process, you will train your attention and concentration to remain more focused and less distractible. By continuing to practice, you'll learn how not to provide energy to negative thoughts and chronic threat-based thinking, which will allow these thoughts to dissipate. This will help you slow down and reduce your chronic stress.

Breathing

Well over two thousand years ago, Taoist literature pointed out that improper breathing is a problem both physically and psychologically. Improper breathing is rapid, shallow, difficult, and strained. It isn't even or free-flowing. It doesn't originate from our center. It is clearly linked to chronic stress and unhappiness.

In Taoist practices, proper breathing is essential for health, longevity, enjoying life, and removing chronic stress. It's also necessary for spiritual development. Proper breathing, which is fundamental to Taoist meditation, originates from our center and is deep, slow, even, and free-flowing. It is continuous, unbroken, subtle, relaxed, extended, and quiet. Proper breathing takes two primary forms: The first is inhaling through the nose and exhaling through the nose. The second is inhaling through the nose and exhaling through the mouth.

In Taoist practices, attending to and concentrating on the breath refines our breathing. This removes tension and stress from the body, empties the mind of agitation, frees us from entanglement with the affairs of the world, allows us to relax, and unifies body and mind with the universe.

Practice   Awareness of the Breath

For a more experiential understanding of improper and proper breathing, take a few minutes to simply direct your awareness to your breathing. Don't think about it; just focus on it. If you find yourself getting distracted from focusing on your breathing, simply acknowledge that you're distracted without making any judgments about it, then refocus on your breathing. Focus on your breathing for about five minutes. If this seems too long, adjust the time frame to what works best for you.

* * *

Now reflect upon what just happened. What did you notice? What did you feel? Were you inhaling and exhaling through your nose? Did you inhale through your nose and exhale through your mouth? Did you breathe entirely through your mouth? Was your breathing rapid and shallow, or slow and deep? Was it quiet or noisy? Did you find yourself getting distracted? If so, what did you notice about your breathing when you were distracted? Did it change? Were you easily able to refocus on the breath? What happened to your breathing the longer you stayed focused on it? Did you feel more relaxed?

Given the close relationship between breathing and chronic stress, you may want to periodically focus on your breathing throughout the day. When you do so, ask yourself what your breathing patterns are telling you. You may wish to write about some of these experiences in your journal.

Guan

A major cause of chronic stress is preconceived biases, filters, expectations, and judgments about what we unrealistically fear is going to happen and how it will make us feel. In this way, we are negatively impacted by our thoughts long before the feared event has a chance to occur. This threat-based thinking, which generates racing thoughts because of the self-generated and usually unrealistic fear, activates the fight-or-flight response. Then, if we should happen to enter the feared situation, we are already stressed and uncomfortable. This physical and psychological reaction has nothing to do with our actual experience of the situation because we're reacting to what we believe we are going to feel and experience.

Because of our expectations, judgments, and rigid and inflexible threat-based thinking, we are constantly interfering with ourselves. Mind and body are agitated and fragmented. We aren't integrated. As a result, we don't allow ourselves to be in the present, where we can experience and gain insight into the actual situation. Instead, we just stress ourselves out.

The Taoist approach is quite aware of this rigid and inflexible thinking and judging that fragments us, interferes with our ability to actually experience the present, and leads to chronic stress. It advocates guan, or natural observation. This means observing from a detached, unbiased perspective. Practicing guan provides us with insight not only into the world around us, but into the mind and body. It means engaging the world in the present, without the mind galloping all over the place. It means experiencing all aspects of our world without the filter of judgments that lead to chronic stress. As such, it is a way to help reduce chronic stress, since it involves being free of any expectations or judgments about what we are going to feel or experience in the future.

We've all had fleeting moments when our minds weren't agitated, distracted, and racing all over the place. We were fully in the present. We weren't fragmented. For a moment, we weren't chronically stressed. This may have occurred while watching a sunrise or sunset, listening to the birds, listening to music, feeling the wind, going with the flow in some physical activity, or watching and listening to the waves crash on the shore. Our senses were enhanced. We had a feeling, if just for a moment, of being truly alive and integrated with the world around us. Even if we didn't know it, in that moment we were practicing guan.

In Taoism the goal is to develop this perspective, increasing it from occasional mere glimpses to a regular occurrence. Interacting with the world and ourselves through guan is a process that must be developed and cultivated through practice. The aim is to make guan the norm.

It will take time to develop your guan. As you continue to practice regularly, it will become easier to implement and will start to become the norm rather than the exception. At that point your chronic stress will appear to be melting away.

Practice   Eating with Guan

When we eat, we tend to be engaged in multiple tasks in addition to eating. We may be watching TV, listening to the radio, engaged in a conversation, thinking about something, reading something, talking on the phone, working, or driving. Our minds are full and bouncing all over the place. The process of eating is on automatic pilot. We aren't fully engaged with just eating. As a result, we aren't really aware of simply eating in the here and now. We are distracted and fragmented.

In order to reacquaint yourself with your guan and start to cultivate it, the next time you eat something, try to eat with guan. Eating with guan means focusing solely on eating. Don't engage in any other activities while eating. Try to just observe, without any preconceptions, judgments, or biases, whatever occurs in your mind and body as you eat. In a sense, you are a witness to your own eating. As a detached observer, what insights do you discover about eating while you are eating?

Don't worry if you find yourself getting distracted. For most people, maintaining guan is a challenge at first. If you get distracted, simply acknowledge that this has occurred and return to eating. You may need to do this again and again. By nonjudgmentally acknowledging your distraction and returning to eating, you are beginning to train your attention and concentration. You are also beginning to develop guan. This will take time and practice. Let go of any frustrations that may arise about only being able to engage in the process for a brief period of time. This is normal.

Initially, spend just five minutes applying guan to eating. For the remainder of the meal, you can return to eating as you normally do. If you want to go longer, that's fine. If not, that's also fine. You may find it challenging to practice for even one minute. Again, this is normal. Don't dwell on any frustrations that may arise. This process is intended to help you learn about yourself and what you need to do to overcome your stress. Just trying this exercise will provide you with considerable insight.

When you're finished eating, reflect on whatever you noticed happening in your mind and body as you ate with guan. Did you notice a difference in how you felt when you ate with guan as opposed to how you felt when you didn't? Record your experiences and thoughts in your journal.

As previously noted, to develop guan to help you gain insight into and reduce your chronic stress, you must practice on a regular basis. The great thing about guan is that you can apply it to anything you do, wherever you are. Whether eating, taking a shower, going for a walk, washing the dishes, exercising, listening to music, watching the rain, or interacting with others, you can practice guan. During the course of your day, periodically select an activity with which to practice guan for a few moments. Note what you discover about yourself. You might wish to occasionally write about this in your journal.

Smiling and Meditation

There is an additional component of Taoist meditation that's generally overlooked: smiling. When you practice the various meditation techniques you'll learn throughout this book, make sure you smile while performing them. For that matter, throughout your entire day, whenever you find the opportunity to do so, remind yourself to simply smile. Notice how your feelings change immediately—how your mind empties, your body relaxes, and your posture straightens. Observe that you are attentive and focused, your breathing is natural, and you are nonjudgmental and in the present. Be aware that, at least for the moment, your stress is gone. All from a simple smile!

Interlude

At this point, spend a few moments thinking about what you've learned up to this point in the chapter. Also reflect on what you experienced with the various activities and practices you engaged in. What did you discover? Remember, the Taoist path has two interrelated components: the mental and the physical. Both are required. The first half of this chapter focused on the mental; the remainder focuses on the physical component and your subjective awareness.

Qigong

Qigong is a recent term for ancient Taoist practices for making the mind and body healthy. Essentially, the word "qigong" refers to working with qi. If you recall, "qi" refers to both energy and breath. Qigong is all about proper breathing and working with the body and mind so energy circulates without any barriers or impediments. Many of the movements in qigong consist of stretching, twisting, coiling, and uncoiling various parts of the body. These movements relieve physical tension due to chronic stress. Qigong also trains attention and concentration, allowing us to still the mind and release the agitation that causes and maintains chronic stress. The practice of qigong allows us to root and center ourselves while integrating mind, body, and environment into a unified, free-flowing process.

I'll introduce you to two basic types of Taoist qigong: sitting and standing. The sitting form is called Baduanjin, or Eight Pieces of Brocade. You will learn all eight postures of this form. The standing form is called Yijinjing, or the Method of Changing and Transforming the Muscles and Tendons. You will learn eight of the postures from this form. A significant number of the Yijinjing postures are adapted from a more basic qigong practice known as Zhan Zhuang, or Standing like a Tree or Stake in the Ground. Deceptively simple in appearance, Zhan Zhuang is one of the most profound techniques for gaining insight into the workings of the mind and body, eliminating chronic stress, and enhancing overall health and well-being.

As with anything else, to be proficient in qigong and obtain its benefits you need to practice regularly and consistently. Try to perform each posture at least three times a week. Start with five-minute sessions for each one, and increase the duration as you feel more comfortable with them. If need be, you can also start with a shorter duration. Use any method you like to keep track of time.

It's usually best to practice in the mornings, but if this isn't possible, any time that works for you is fine. Find a quiet, comfortable place to practice where you won't be disturbed. Each time you practice, spend a few moments recording what you did and describing your experiences in your journal. Review what you've written about your practice once a week.

Practice   Posture 1 of the Baduanjin Sequence: Sitting in Stillness

Find a room or other place that's quiet and where you won't be disturbed for at least five minutes. Simply sit on the floor. You can use a flat cushion or pillow if you like. Cross your legs at the ankles and pull them in toward your body. If your knees can touch the floor, let them do so. If not, it's perfectly okay for them to be off the floor. If this position is a problem for you, it's okay to sit on a chair, but make sure both of your feet are flat on the floor.

Imagine the top of your head being gently pulled up by a string. As you do so, your back will naturally align in the correct posture, like a plant that's being drawn toward the sun and rooted down into the ground at the same time. Your spine, maintaining its natural curve, will straighten but not be tight or tense. Look directly forward, and then gently close your eyes. Closing your eyes eliminates visual distractions. Relax your shoulders and allow a small space in your armpits; it may help to imagine that you have a golf ball in each armpit. Hold your hands flat or in loosely coiled fists and allow them to rest gently on your upper thighs or in your lap. Your mouth should be closed, with your teeth gently touching each other and your tongue touching the roof of your mouth. Relax.

Remember natural observation, or guan, and apply it while practicing the posture Sitting in Stillness. Perform a quick scan of your body, taking just a minute or so to observe your body using guan. Remember to smile. Begin with your feet, noting what you observe, and gradually move upward, observing your lower legs, thighs, pelvic area, buttocks, abdomen, back, chest, shoulders, arms, hands, neck, and head, in that order.

When you've finished, redirect your attention to your breathing, gently noticing your inhalation and exhalation. Breathe in and out through your nose. Then take a deep, slow, quiet, long, relaxed, and continuous breath through your nose. Deep breathing requires the activation of your diaphragm, which will result in your abdomen expanding outward while you inhale. Once you've inhaled fully, simply release your abdomen and exhale slowly and naturally through your nose. Breathe in this way a few more times, until you feel comfortable with it. This deep abdominal breathing will allow you to naturally find

35

your center and relax into it. When you feel comfortable, continue following your breath for five more minutes, naturally observing and noting in your mind whatever you observe. Remember to smile.

If you get distracted, as often happens, don't let it bother you. Keep smiling. As in the exercise Eating with Guan, simply acknowledge the distraction nonjudgmentally and then refocus on your breathing. You're likely to find yourself getting distracted more than once. Again, this is perfectly normal. Just continue to acknowledge the distraction and return to your breathing.

When you finish the exercise but before opening your eyes, scan your body as you did before, moving sequentially upward from your feet to your head. Also quickly scan your mind. Then open your eyes and wait a few minutes before getting up to allow yourself to return to your environment. If you've been sitting cross-legged, also stretch your legs out before you get up. As you transition out of the exercise, observe your breath, following your inhalations and exhalations and mentally noting whatever you observe.

Take some time to record and describe your experiences with Sitting in Stillness in your journal. Describe whatever you remember happening in your mind and body. Don't force it; just reflect upon it. Did you notice a difference between the first body scan and the second? Did you feel any different? What are your body and mind telling you about yourself? This will provide you with information and insights about what you need to change in order to eliminate chronic stress. You may wish to mark this page in the book, as I recommend that you reflect on your experience and write in your journal in a similar way after learning each new posture.

Practice   Posture 1 of the Yijinjing Sequence: Wuji Standing

Stand straight, with your feet parallel and together and your knees slightly bent and in line with your toes. Your weight should be evenly distributed on both feet. Imagine that the top of your head is being gently pulled up, like a puppet by a string. As you do so, your lower body will sink and your back will naturally align in the correct posture, like a plant that's being drawn toward the sun and rooted down into the ground at the same time. Your spine will be straight but not tight or tense. Keep your eyes open and look forward. Your mouth should be closed, with your teeth gently touching each other. Let your arms hang down naturally alongside your body, with your palms facing your thighs. Let your shoulders hang down. For this exercise, breathe naturally, inhaling and exhaling through your nose. Don't be concerned about diaphragmatic breathing; just breathe through your nose as you normally would. Relax, smile, practice guan, and simply note what you feel in your mind and body.

Let your attention wander through your body as you stand. Unlike in Sitting in Stillness, don't focus on your breath unless you find yourself distracted. If you do get distracted, simply accept that you got distracted, don't make any judgments about it, and focus on your breathing for two or three breaths to center yourself and quiet your mind. Then return your attention to your body and mind and note what you feel. Cultivate the perspective of being a detached witness to what's occurring in your mind and body as you stand. Try to do this exercise for five minutes. If you feel uncomfortable or dizzy while performing this exercise, stop, get a drink of water, and sit down for a few minutes. Return to the practice when you feel settled and comfortable.

When you're finished, reflect upon and write in your journal about what happened to you as you practiced Wuji Standing. How did you feel when you finished the exercise? Did you feel relaxed? Were you able to stand straight and keep a stable posture? Did you find yourself moving around? Did you feel rooted in the ground? Did you feel centered? Did you sense any movement, pulsating, tingling, heaviness, warmth, lightness, or flowing, like water through a hose, in your body? If so, this is normal. These kinds of descriptions are often used to describe the feeling of qi moving throughout your body. Again, you may wish to mark this page and use this paragraph for guidance in writing in your journal as you learn each new posture in the Yijinjing sequence.

Essentially, Wuji Standing is a Taoist practice for acquainting you with your body and mind. What usually occurs when people first practice this exercise is that they notice tightness, stiffness, minor aches and pains, and sensations of being uncomfortable in various parts of the body. This is normal. If you experience this, it's just your body letting you know that there are some problems you need to address. Another common experience is that people are easily distracted or bored and complain about being stuck in their head. This is also normal. If you experience this, your mind is letting you know that there are problems with your attention and concentration.

At this early stage in your practice, the most important aspect of this technique is what you learn about yourself when you apply guan during the practice. Wuji Standing provides you with information about what you need to change in order to eliminate chronic stress.

Conclusion

At this point, you should have a fairly good idea of the basic components of Taoist meditation techniques and how the practices are performed. Give them a chance to work for you. Remember guan. Try to apply it whenever and wherever you can. Remember to smile whenever you can. You'll notice a profound difference in yourself and your life if you do so. Building on the basis established in this chapter, let's now move forward into the first component of the Taoist path: simplifying life.

Part 2

Simplifying Your Life

Chapter 3

Simplifying Your Thoughts

In Taoism, the more complex our lives, the greater the likelihood that we'll suffer from chronic stress. Thus, across all forms of Taoism, simplifying life is of fundamental importance for eliminating chronic stress, and also for spiritual development. Simplifying life includes both mental and physical approaches, which are intertwined like yin and yang and cannot be separated. This chapter focuses on the Taoist path of simplifying life by simplifying our thoughts, including beliefs and judgments. In order to do this, of course, we first need to be aware of our thoughts, and then we need to examine them to determine which should be simplified or eliminated. This is an application of guan.

The Galloping Mind

In the previous chapter, you learned about the Taoist notion of galloping while sitting. This refers to our high degree of distractibility and our problems with attention and concentration—difficulties that result in a continually agitated mind that gallops all over the place.

Because the continually agitated mind is filled with absolute concepts, beliefs, expectations, judgments, biases, and perspectives that gallop, seemingly out of control, across our mental landscape, its thinking is quite rigid and complex. The more rigid and complex our thinking, the greater the likelihood that we will perceive threats to our perspectives on life. Thus, rigid thinking not only initiates the fight-or-flight response, but also keeps it activated, leading to chronic stress.

To eliminate this chronic stress, we need to remove the complexity and rigidness of our thinking. We need to simplify our thinking. This removes the clutter from the mind. In this way, we begin to simplify our lives.

Although the previous chapter provided an experiential introduction to wandering mind in the context of meditative practices, it didn't give you a good opportunity to experience it in a nonmeditative context. You weren't exposed to all the clutter in your mind. The next exercise will remedy that.

Practice   Observing Your Thoughts

In this exercise you'll explore what exactly the *Zhuangzi* refers to as galloping while sitting. Find a place where you can be alone and sit comfortably for ten minutes without any outside distractions. Turn off your TV, radio, cell phone, iPod, and other potentially distracting devices. Get a timer and set it for ten minutes.

For the full ten minutes, just sit and don't think about anything. Don't try to focus on one thing, such as your breath, a body part, or a word. This isn't a meditation. I don't want you to meditate. Just sit and don't think about anything. When your timer goes off, stop.

*   *   *

What happened? What did you notice? Did you get distracted by anything? Did thoughts almost immediately begin to pop up even though you were trying not to think? Did your thoughts connect to other thoughts, seemingly on their own, such that you found yourself talking to yourself in your head about something? Were you wondering about the exercise? Did you find yourself making negative judgments about it? Did you find that your mind was galloping all over the place? If so, this is normal; it's what most people experience.

The purpose of this exercise is to simply make you aware of your racing thoughts and demonstrate that, at this point, you don't have as much control over your thoughts as you probably think you do. In

Taoism this agitated mind, with its galloping thoughts, is seen as the primary source of chronic stress.

Our Changing World

As mentioned in chapter 2, in Taoism, existence is seen as a continual, cyclic process of change. Taoists accept change and the uncertainty associated with it as natural. The goal of Taoism is to be in harmony with this natural process of change. This requires us to be flexible and adaptable. It also requires that our thoughts and beliefs be consistent with our ever-changing world. Unfortunately, for most of us this isn't the case.

In general, most of us don't like change and uncertainty, especially regarding events, conditions, people, and objects that are meaningful to us. Uncertainty is threatening because we feel we don't have control over the situation or ourselves. Insofar as this is threatening, it activates the fight-or-flight response and we become stressed. We don't like the uncomfortable feelings associated with this stress.

In order to address these unpleasant feelings, we build a rigid and complex worldview composed of absolute concepts, beliefs, expectations, judgments, biases, and perspectives. These essentially serve to deny change and uncertainty. While this is functional to a point, if something occurs that violates our absolute expectations about how we, others, and the world should behave, we feel threatened because the change and the uncertainty associated with it are staring us in the face. Our rigid and complex worldview is no longer protecting us. In fact, it has become a source of chronic stress because there's a mismatch between our thinking, which is absolute and unchanging, and the world around us, which is characterized by a continual, cyclic process of change.

The Zhuangzi and Change

One of the earliest Taoist texts to address thoughts, beliefs, and judgments about change and the uncertainty associated with it and examine them at the most basic level was the *Zhuangzi*, written over 2,200 years ago. Unlike many other texts of the time, the *Zhuangzi* presented a number of its teachings through stories and tales. One such story from chapter 18 (Guo 1974) offers a teaching about absolute expectations, the continual process of change, and how to address it within the context of the most stressful of all experiences: death.

Zhuangzi's wife had died. His good friend Huizi had come to show his respect and express his condolences. Upon his arrival, Huizi saw Zhuangzi sitting on the floor with his legs spread apart, beating on a basin and singing. For Huizi, this behavior was totally inappropriate and violated all expectations regarding rituals and correct conduct for mourning. Clearly upset, he confronted Zhuangzi and said, "You have lived together, raised children, and grown old. That you do not weep is one thing. But beating a basin and singing, isn't that going too far?"

Zhuangzi replied, "Not so! When she first died, I did mourn and express my feelings. Upon examining her beginnings, she originally was without life. Not moving, without life, originally without form. Not moving, without form, originally without vital energy or qi. Undifferentiated! Suddenly, within the obscurity a change occurs and there is qi. Qi changes and there is form. Form changes and there is life. Now, another change and there is death. This is the movement of the four seasons. If I followed those who shouted and wept, I would consider myself as not being open to my destiny. Thus, I stopped!"

Prior to visiting Zhuangzi, Huizi had already made up his mind about how he should feel and behave when somebody died. He wasn't allowing himself to feel and behave as a direct result of a here-and-now experience. He also believed that Zhuangzi must behave according to his, Huizi's, absolute expectations regarding rituals and correct conduct for mourning. When Zhuangzi didn't behave as expected, Huizi's absolute perspective was threatened. In order to eliminate the resulting unpleasant feelings and reestablish his own absolute perspective, Huizi confronted Zhuangzi with his absolute negative judgments regarding Zhuangzi's behavior.

Zhuangzi, on the other hand, who had lost his wife, was in the here and now. Initially, Zhuangzi expressed his feelings about his loss. His feeling of sadness was a direct result of his wife dying. He felt sad because that was how he actually felt, not because it was how he was supposed to feel.

Zhuangzi's subsequent thinking was consistent with his experience of the here-and-now. Zhuangzi had simplified his thoughts, beliefs, and judgments regarding change and death by becoming aware of them, examining them, and then letting go of his rigid and complex worldview. The story points out that by changing and simplifying our thinking, we can change how we feel and behave. This entire process is the application of guan.

Practice   Experiencing Change

While we can initially talk about accepting change from a cognitive perspective, for Taoists change must eventually be experienced directly. In chapter 16 of the *Daodejing* (Wang 1993), the author directly observes, through the practice of guan, that all things continually interact and move in cycles. In order to experience this, we need to practice guan. Simply find a place to sit—in a mall, at a park, at the beach, or wherever you like. Then sit and just observe for about ten minutes in a detached, nonjudgmental manner (with guan) all the changes that occur around you. Just experience your environment without thinking about it.

Upon finishing this practice, note what you observed. Were you able to experience continual change no matter where you looked? Now think about the discussion of change you've read in this chapter. Do you notice the difference between talking about change as fundamental and actually experiencing continual change as fundamental? If you like, you can record your thoughts and feelings in your journal.

Beliefs

Our beliefs help us create and live in our personal and social reality. They assist us in looking at, organizing, making judgments about, and responding to our personal and social worlds. We all have beliefs that guide us through our daily challenges and decisions. In most cases, our beliefs are beneficial to our everyday living. In some cases, though, our beliefs are problematic and can lead to unhealthy consequences, including chronic stress.

In this section I'll provide two examples of how problematic beliefs and the associated judgments can negatively impact feelings and behavior, resulting in chronic stress. The first example is from that ancient Taoist text the *Liezi* (Yang 1972). The second is a modern situation that may have a ring of familiarity for you.

A Man and His Hometown

There was a man who was born in the state of Yan. Upon his birth, his family moved to the state of Chu. When he grew old, he wanted to return to see his birthplace in the state of Yan. Because he did not know how to get there, some people he knew said they would show him the way. While they were passing though the state of Jin, his traveling companions deceived him. They pointed toward a town and told him that it was his place of birth in the state of Yan. His hometown. The man's appearance immediately changed and he looked sad. His companions then led him to a building and said, "This is the home of your ancestors." Tears dripped down his face as he wept. They then indicated a ridge and said, "This is the graveyard of your ancestors." The man couldn't keep from sobbing.

Then his traveling companions laughed loudly and said, "We have been deceiving you all along. This is the state of Jin." The man felt ashamed. When they actually reached the state of Yan and he enteredthe town where he had really been born, saw the home of his ancestors, and the graveyard of his ancestors, he felt only slight sadness in his heart.

Because of his absolute judgment, based on his absolute belief that the first city was his hometown, the man cried and felt sad with no basis in fact. He cried and felt sad because he believed he was in his hometown and believed that this was how he was supposed to behave when he returned to his place of birth and the home of his ancestors. Once he was presented with evidence that he wasn't in his hometown, his beliefs changed. And as a result of that, his feelings and behavior changed. When he finally reached his real hometown and engaged with it on an experiential level, without any expectations about how he was supposed to feel, his behavior and feelings were different and more natural.

This story clearly indicates how beliefs and judgments can determine our reality and influence how we feel and behave. It also demonstrates how beliefs and the expectations based on them can lead to distress. Clearly, it is important to become aware of, examine, and then remove beliefs and judgments that are detrimental to us. In this way, we begin to simplify our lives.

Jane's Story

One Monday morning while Jane was combing her hair in front of the mirror, she noticed a brownish spot at the base of her hairline. She rubbed her finger over it. She thought it felt flat but wasn't sure and wondered if it might be raised. She looked closely at it. It didn't appear to be irregular in shape, but as she examined it, she thought it might look a bit irregular around the edges. She thought, *Oh my god, is this a skin cancer? You can die from skin cancer!* She started to tense up and felt a cold sweat. Her stomach was uneasy. It was too early in the morning to call for an appointment to see a doctor. Her mind spun, wondering what to do.

Jane went to her computer and searched online for information about brown spots on the forehead. She saw pictures on a number of sites that resembled the spot she had on her forehead. These sites called it an age spot or liver spot and said it was a harmless effect of excessive sun exposure. Nevertheless, she thought, *I couldn't be so lucky. I bet it is a cancer!*

So she searched for the term "skin cancer" and once again found an endless number of sites. The more she looked at pictures on site after site, the stronger her belief that she had skin cancer became. She felt the spot over and over and decided it was raised. The more she looked at it, the more it looked irregular, both in shape and at the edges. Her breathing became rapid and shallow. Her mouth got quite dry, and her thoughts began to race: *It's a melanoma! I don't want to die. What am I going to do?*

Jane looked up at the clock and saw that it was now late enough that her doctor's office would be open. She immediately called and told the nurse that she thought she had a melanoma and wanted to make an appointment for that day. The nurse said the doctor was booked up until the end of the week, but there was a dermatologist in the building, who was more qualified to see her for this concern anyway. Jane contacted the dermatologist's office and made an appointment for the first time slot available—a few days later at 3 p.m.

For the entire time until she saw the doctor, Jane believed she had a melanoma and that the worst was going to happen. She shared her concern with her friends and family, and although everyone believed she just had an age spot, they couldn't sway her from believing it was cancerous. She became locked in a negative loop as her absolute beliefs resulted in insomnia, loss of appetite, high anxiety, tension, and hardly being able to think about anything else. She was so stressed by her belief that she called in sick to work.

After Jane arrived at the doctor's office, the intensity of her stress increased because she believed that once the doctor saw the spot on her forehead, he would confirm her fear. Finally, she was taken to an exam room. A few minutes later, the doctor walked in, introduced himself, and looked at the spot. Then he looked at it again through a huge magnifying glass. He told Jane it was an age spot and that she had nothing to worry about. To say Jane felt relieved would be an understatement. He also told her she had been smart to come in to have him look at it.

Most of us have been in situations where we were waiting for a doctor's response about symptoms, a blood test, a biopsy, an X-ray, and so on. In most cases, we worry about it to a certain degree. Uncertainty creates anxiety. This is normal.

However, when we have an absolute, threat-based belief, we can end up harming ourselves, even though there may be no information to support that belief. Once Jane arrived at an absolute belief that she had a melanoma, her fight-or-flight response was activated, and she kept it activated with her ongoing threat-based thinking. As a result she was chronically stressed, and the stress was so severe that it interfered with her sleep, eating, physical health, and emotional well-being.

Practice   Examining Your Beliefs

Both of the preceding stories point out how absolute beliefs and judgments can complicate life, create stress, and be both physically and psychologically harmful. The antidote is to simplify your life by changing or removing absolute beliefs and judgments that cause you stress. This exercise will help you discover and explore your own problematic absolute beliefs and judgments, which is the first step in getting rid of them.

Simply take some time to think about situations in your life where your absolute beliefs and judgments created problems. Did these thoughts cause the problem or make it worse? Did they make a straightforward situation much more complex and stressful? Do you still have these rigid and inflexible thoughts? In your journal, list these problematic absolute beliefs and judgments. Try to come up with at least five. For each one, describe the problems they caused or exacerbated. Then ask yourself why you still hold these absolute beliefs and judgments.

Two Simple Taoist Guidelines

Guidelines are beliefs, thoughts, and concepts that focus, direct, and motivate our behavior and assist us in solving various problems in an efficient and effective manner. In Taoism, it's crucial to understand that change is fundamental, that we need to be flexible, and that we need to eliminate problematic absolute thoughts, judgments, and beliefs. It is important to note that Taoist teachings about thinking are always directly related to feelings and behaviors. The two are intimately interconnected. Not only do we need to eliminate problematic thoughts, judgments, and beliefs, we also need to replace them with stress-reducing thoughts, judgments, and beliefs, which will have positive effects on our behavior.

Two basic Taoist guidelines regarding the relationship between thinking and behavior relative to reducing stress are believing in and respecting oneself, and practicing moderation. Following these guidelines will help you simplify not only your thinking, but also your life. As a result, they can help ease chronic stress. The following two stories demonstrate how these Taoist guidelines are manifested in behaviors that prevent or reduce chronic stress.

Believing in and Respecting Oneself

The workload at Veronica's office was quite intense and sometimes overwhelming. In recent months, two of her coworkers had been terminated, but Veronica kept her job because she did good work in an efficient and effective manner, didn't doubt herself, didn't waste time whining, took responsibility for her behavior, was flexible, and loved a challenge.

Veronica believed in herself and operated with an attitude of "I can!" In contrast, the two people who were let go didn't work efficiently and effectively, constantly doubted themselves, whined a lot, tended to avoid responsibility, and were rigid. Basically, they operated with an attitude of "I can't!"

Although Veronica made very few mistakes, she certainly wasn't perfect. But on the rare occasions when she made mistakes, she didn't lose respect for herself or doubt or chastise herself. She learned from her mistakes, corrected them, and then moved forward. As a result, she didn't stress herself out.

Veronica also exhibited flexibility by knowing her limits and adapting to challenges in her environment. When she faced a task that was a bit beyond her current skill level, she didn't take an attitude of "I can't!" Rather, her attitude was "I need assistance so I can learn how to do this." When she faced a task that was significantly beyond her current skill level, she simply passed it on to someone capable of doing it. In those cases, she didn't think of herself as a failure, lose respect for herself, or doubt herself. Rather, she continued to respect and believe in herself. In this way, too, she didn't stress herself out.

Practicing Moderation

Arthur was at least thirty pounds overweight. He didn't exercise. His eating behaviors were excessive, and his exercise behaviors were deficient. Maria, on the other hand, was at least twenty pounds underweight and seemed to exercise all the time. Her eating behaviors were deficient, and her exercise behaviors were excessive.

Although outwardly they appeared very different, both Arthur and Maria experienced significant physical and mental stress as a result of their excessive and deficient behaviors, which were linked to problematic thoughts, judgments, and beliefs. Both experienced unpleasant symptoms that caused them to see their doctors. In both cases, their doctors recommended a simple guideline to address their problem: moderation— not being excessive or deficient in their eating and exercise behavior. Both were provided with information and resources offering guidance on eating, exercise, and stress management.

Because both of them were tired of their chronic stress, they accepted the advice to practice moderation and chose to believe in themselves. As a result, both had an "I can!" attitude and were able to change their stress-producing behavior. Arthur began eating less, while Maria began eating more. Arthur started exercising, while Maria dialed back her exercise regimen. Changing their thoughts and beliefs resulted in a change of behaviors and lifestyle.

Taoists believe in practicing moderation in all aspects of life. In fact, in Taoism finding the balance point between excessiveness and deficiency constitutes harmony (Guanzi 2012).

Interlude

As first noted in the previous chapter, each chapter has a mental, or rationally focused, component and a physical, experiential component, consisting of qigong practice. The mentally based component of this chapter focused on how chronic threat-based thinking (problematic thoughts, beliefs, and judgments) agitates the mind and creates and maintains chronic stress. It also examined how simplifying life by rationally changing or eliminating problematic thoughts, beliefs, and judgments can be helpful in calming the mind and thus removing chronic stress.

The physical qigong component, which composes the remainder of this chapter, has the same goal: removing chronic stress by changing or eliminating chronic threat-based thinking. However, it does so via a completely different pathway: relaxing the body. When you simply and solely focus on the physical practices, the body will naturally relax because you aren't subject to threat-based thinking. This being the case, the mind isn't agitated and begins to relax. Through consistent and regular practice, chronic threat-based thinking naturally fades away, allowing chronic stress to dissipate.

Qigong

As noted in chapter 2, all of the postures in both Baduanjin (the sitting form) and Yijinjing (the standing form) are part of a sequence and an ongoing practice. Each new movement flows from the previous movement. To build each qigong sequence, first learn the new posture. Then go through the sequence, beginning with the first posture and linking all the postures you've learned thus far in a continuous series. Because you will have been practicing the preceding movements in each form, the transition into the new posture should be straightforward. Throughout, work on developing and improving the five basics—posture, attention, concentration, breathing, and guan—with all the postures of both Baduanjin and Yijinjing. Also remember to smile!

Upon finishing each two-posture sequence, reflect on what you experienced while performing it. What are your body and mind telling you about yourself? Are you starting to feel rooted and centered? Take some time to write in your journal, describing what occurred while you performed these movements.

Practice   Posture 2 of the Baduanjin Sequence: Gently Clicking Your Teeth and Embracing Kunlun Mountain

Having completed the first movement, Sitting in Stillness, remain seated with your back straight, head pulled up, legs crossed, and hands on your upper thighs or lap. In other words, stay in the Sitting in Stillness form.

The second posture has two parts. The first part is to keep your lips gently closed and softly click your teeth together thirty-six times by striking your top teeth with your bottom teeth. After the thirty-sixth click, rotate your tongue in a counterclockwise direction across your outer gums three times. Then repeat in the opposite direction, running your tongue over your outer gums in a clockwise direction three times. At this point, you should feel saliva in your mouth. Swish it all around your mouth. Then swallow it in three noisy gulps. Visualize it entering your lower dantian.

For the second part of this posture, bring your hands up in front of your chest, about twelve inches from your chest, with your palms touching each other, fingers facing up and elbows pointing down. Rub your palms and fingers together until you feel some heat. Next, clasp your fingers together and put them on the back of your head just above your ears with your elbows gently pulled back. Keeping your back and neck straight, inhale deeply through your nose while gently bending your head slightly forward, bringing your elbows inward, and softly pushing on the back of your head with your hands. Exhale through your mouth and gently pull your head and elbows back to their original position. You should feel the pressure of your hands pushing your head forward while your neck muscles pull your head back to its original position. This completes one repetition. Repeat this eight more times, for a total of nine repetitions. After completing the ninth repetition, let your hands return to their original position so that you are once again in the Sitting in Stillness position.

When you get stressed-out, the muscles in your neck become tense. The second part of this posture (Embracing Kunlun Mountain, which is the head movement) helps relieve tension in the neck while simultaneously strengthening its muscles. The clicking of your teeth should clear your mind. The swallowing of saliva is believed to aid digestion. Visualizing the saliva entering the lower dantian helps you develop your center and still your mind.

Practice Posture 2 of the Yijinjing Sequence: Holding a Ball in Front of Your Chest

Upon finishing the Wuji Standing movement, step to the left so your feet are shoulder-width apart and simply raise both of your arms, palms facing each other, in a forward and upward arc until your palms are chest high. Then bring your fingertips toward each other until they are almost touching. Your hands should be in line with the center of your chest. It will look as though your arms are encircling a large ball. Keep your shoulders relaxed and down, and angle your elbows downward and to the sides. Breathe naturally. Stay in this position for one to two minutes. Smile and practice guan.

By changing your hand position from the Wuji position to the position Holding a Ball in Front of Your Chest, you allow your body to communicate with you from a different configuration. This helps you become more aware of your body and develops your ability to listen to your body. What is it telling you?

Conclusion

This chapter focused on simplifying your thinking—one aspect of simplifying your life, which is one of the three components of the Taoist path. To help you simplify your thinking, it focused on removing clutter from your mind, embracing the reality of continual change, examining your beliefs, and exploring some basic Taoist guidelines for interacting with the world. In Taoism, which is quite practical in its approach to being in harmony with life, thinking must always be linked with behavior. The next chapter explores this link.

Chapter 4

Simplifying Your Behavior

In the Taoist view, to eliminate chronic stress we need to remove our problematic behaviors, as our thinking and behavior are intimately linked and reinforce each other. In most cases, our behavior expresses our thoughts. Problematic thoughts give rise to problematic behaviors, which then help create and maintain chronic stress. Removing these behaviors helps ease stress and also has the benefit of decreasing our behavioral options. This simplifies our behavioral choices, and therefore simplifies life.

Eating, Drinking, Sleeping, and Exercising Behavior

The Taoist path is focused on making life as stress-free as possible by behaving in a simple and straightforward manner. Four basic areas that are often compromised by problematic behavior that results in chronic stress are eating, drinking, sleeping, and exercise. There are numerous Taoist texts that address these areas (Kohn 2012). Because these aspects of life are so important to overall well-being, I will also discuss them in chapter 5, in the context of noninterference, and in chapter 6, in the context of desires.

Taoism has long been aware that how we eat and drink, what we eat and drink, and how much or how little we eat and drink can have a significant impact on our overall health. Within Taoism, certain foods and beverages are considered to be medicinal and beneficial for our overall well-being (Kohn 2010a; Saso 1994). The *Neiye* (Guanzi 2012) is quite clear that excessive or deficient eating and drinking compromise the flow of qi and are detrimental to your well-being. The *Yangxing Yanming Lu* (*Nourishing Your Nature and Extending Your Life*), a seventh-century text on health and longevity, attributes much of illness and unnatural death to what we eat and drink (Tao Hongming 2013). In other words, your diet can lead to chronic stress and thus harm you.

Likewise, Taoism recognizes that we all need consistent, restful sleep and advocates going to bed early and rising early in the morning (*Neijing* 2007). Inadequate or poor-quality sleep compromises physical and psychological health, energy levels, and performance in general. From the perspective of Taoism, problems getting to sleep or staying asleep, not getting enough sleep, or sleeping too much are seen as usually being due to problematic behavior prior to going to bed. This problematic behavior causes stress, which in turn compromises sleep, which leads to further stress due to lack of adequate restful sleep. This creates a vicious cycle that leads to chronic stress.

Finally, Taoism also has a long history of using exercise as a way of curing and preventing illness and disease. The *Neijing* (2007) indicates the importance of stretching, walking, and then cooling down. The *Taiqing Daoyin Yangsheng Jing* (*The Great Clarity Scripture of Guiding and Stretching to Nourish Life*) is a foundational text in this area (Baike 2007). This seventh-century Taoist text presents specific, organized exercise sequences that focus on guiding qi, stretching and relaxing the body and mind, and thereby establishing health and well-being (Kohn 2008a). *Daoyin* and *yangsheng*, both first mentioned in the *Zhuangzi*, are ancient names for practices concerned with health, well-being, and longevity. The term we use today for these practices is "qigong."

The *Yangxing Yanming Lu* clearly presents the Taoist holistic approach to healing, health, and well-being. It integrates guidelines on numerous behaviors—diet, sleep, exercise, meditation, breathing exercises, and sex—not only as a way of taking care of one's body and mind, extending one's life, and eliminating what we now call chronic stress, but also as a precursor to spiritual development and discovery.

Emilio's Story

Emilio, a sophomore in college, had problems with his digestion. He always seemed to have heartburn, stomachaches, gas, and constipation or diarrhea. He couldn't understand why. One day at lunch in the college cafeteria, he didn't see any of his friends, so he sat at a table where an unfamiliar student was eating his lunch. Emilio said a cursory hello to his tablemate, and then he pulled out his phone, made a call, and talked to a friend while he ate lunch.

The other student, Kapena, was having a stir-fry, which he ate slowly with chopsticks. After finishing his meal, he leisurely drank a big glass of water. Meanwhile, Emilio gobbled down a large burger, French fries, and a piece of chocolate cake, gulping down a twenty-four-ounce soda and talking on his phone all the while.

After finishing his phone call and taking his last bite of cake, which he chased with his last gulp of soda, Emilio grasped his belly and started to complain that his stomach hurt. Looking across at Kapena, he said, "I just don't understand. Why does this happen every time I eat? I always seem to get a stomachache, indigestion, and gas. I don't get it!"

Kapena responded by saying, "I might be able to offer some advice if you like, but I'd want to ask you some questions first. Would that be all right?"

Emilio, who was grimacing with pain, said, "No problem. Sure. Anything to stop this!"

Kapena asked, "Do you always eat and drink like you did just now—eating quickly, not really chewing very much, and gulping down soda?"

Emilio replied, "I never really thought about it, but yes, I guess I do."

Then Kapena asked, "Do you often talk on the phone while eating?"

Emilio nodded and said, "Yes. Or if I'm not on the phone, I usually do something else, like watching TV or reading. I always do something while I eat. It saves time!"

Kapena said, "Okay. I think I have some advice for you if you're still interested." Emilio said he was, so Kapena continued.

"Your eating behaviors aren't beneficial for digesting your food. They all stress your body, which results in digestion problems."

Emilio responded, "Yep. You nailed it. How do you know so much about this?"

Kapena replied, "My family has a long history of trying to live in harmony with the ocean, the mountains, and the land, which we can talk about later if you wish. Anyhow, one of our guidelines is that we practice moderation in all of our behaviors. Looking at it that way, your eating behaviors are too excessive. As a result, your body isn't in harmony, or, to use more familiar language, it's overly stressed. This is probably why you have all these symptoms."

Emilio thought about this for a minute, and then said, "Okay. And your advice?"

Kapena said, "You need to slow down and take your time when eating. Chew your food slowly and thoroughly before swallowing it. It's best not to drink while eating. Drink after you finish eating. Also, don't do anything else while you eat and drink. Just eat and drink. Finally, you should probably consider changing how much you eat and drink, and maybe what you eat and drink. I suspect that you don't drink enough water. Most of all, just remember to be moderate in regard to eating and drinking."

Sophia's Story

After getting home from work at around 6 p.m., Sophia typically turned on all the lights in her house, made a pot of coffee, and watched soap operas for two hours, usually drinking two to three cups of coffee as she watched. She often didn't start preparing dinner until 8 p.m. at the earliest, so she often ate around 9 p.m. As she ate, she usually watched a crime drama and drank more coffee. At 10 p.m., she watched another crime show while eating a big bowl of ice cream. Once that show was over at 11 p.m., she watched the news for an hour. Around midnight, she turned off all the lights and headed to bed.

After tossing and turning for about an hour, Sophia usually fell asleep. But she often woke up in the middle of the night feeling hungry, and when that happened, she usually got up and had a snack. After getting back to sleep, she usually slept until her alarm went off. However, she frequently woke up with a headache and felt tired, drained, and a little edgy. This had been going on for a month or so and had resulted in her being late for work on numerous occasions. When she finally got to work on one particular morning, late once again, her boss said, "The next time you come to work late, you'll be fired."

The basic Taoist guideline of moderation is clearly relevant in this situation. Sophia's caffeine consumption is clearly excessive, especially for the evening hours. She could also afford to eat dinner earlier, dim or turn off the lights in the evening, watch more relaxing shows, and avoid television altogether for a while before bed.

William's Story

William was chronically stressed. He tended to overeat and seldom exercised, and he often felt anxious and had trouble sleeping. Lately, his mind seemed to be racing all over the place and he couldn't focus. His body was going downhill, and his job performance was suffering. He recognized that he had a problem and wanted to get his life back on track, but he didn't know how. He noticed that one of his coworkers, a woman named Hua Li, always seemed to be energetic, focused, and happy. She also appeared to be quite athletic. Over lunch one day, he explained his problems and said he felt like he was chronically stressed. He said that he'd noticed how upbeat, calm, and healthy she seemed and asked her what her secret was.

Hua Li smiled and said, "The first step is recognizing that you have a problem and wanting to fix it, and you've done that. Every journey begins with the first step, and by reaching out to me, you're already on your way." That sounded so reassuring that William smiled, heaved a big sigh, and relaxed a bit then and there. Hua Li then said, "The next step is fixing. You do this by changing behaviors that aren't beneficial for your health and well-being." She explained that she was a Taoist and followed Taoism's holistic approach to health and well-being. She also said that she taught a class in qigong and taijiquan, which can help create more balance in life, and invited him to attend. Finally, she recommended a few websites offering information on the Taoist approach.

When William visited the websites, he was intrigued by their emphasis on cultivating the body through stretching, exercise, and meditation and the idea that calming the body could calm the mind. He decided to attend Hua Li's class and was delighted to discover that, in addition to teaching qigong and taijiquan, she discussed the Taoist holistic approach to managing chronic stress. He had known that he needed to make changes in many areas, and here was one cohesive philosophy that addressed sleep, diet, exercise, stretching, meditation, and even interpersonal relationships and being in harmony with the world. He was hooked.

William started his journey by implementing a new routine that involved stretching, exercise, and meditation. Consistent with Taoist teachings, he kept it very simple. Every morning he woke up at 6 a.m. and took a few sips of water. Then he practiced sitting Baduanjin, which begins and ends with meditation and incorporates a series of stretching postures in between. Then he drank some more water and went out for a brisk two-mile walk, followed by a brief cooldown and drinking some more water. After that he ate breakfast and went to work. Three nights a week he attended Hua Li's class.

William noticed that simply changing his morning routine led to many other changes. He started eating more moderately and choosing more healthful foods. And because he now awoke at 6 a.m. daily, he went to bed earlier. He also slept more soundly and felt more rested upon waking. In addition, he noticed that he had more energy, was more focused, and no longer felt anxious. Best of all, he simply felt more alive.

Mildred's Story

One day at work, Sam and his coworker Penny, both parents of teenagers, got into a discussion about how to discipline kids when they talk back. Overhearing their discussion, Mildred, a middle-aged woman who didn't have children, walked over and told them they were both wrong. She went on to tell them the "correct" way to discipline children in this situation. Both Sam and Penny disagreed with her and told her so. Irritated, Mildred pushed the issue by telling them they weren't listening to her.

Penny asked Mildred, "Since you don't have children, how could you possibly know the correct way to stop them from talking back?"

This further irritated Mildred, who responded by saying, "You don't have to have children to know how to raise them properly." Sam was visibly angry and asked her to leave. This infuriated Mildred, and she continued to insist that they were wrong and she was right. Penny, who was extremely exasperated by this point, walked over to Mildred and told her to leave. Mildred, who was starting to shake, clenched her teeth, turned around, and stomped back to her desk.

For the rest of the workday and on her way home, Mildred ruminated about her encounter with Sam and Penny. By the time she got home that night, she was a physical and emotional wreck. She was breathing rather quickly and had a headache and an upset stomach. Her neck, shoulders, and back hurt, and she felt tense all over, anxious, and drained. She was clearly quite stressed.

Around 9 p.m., Mildred's phone rang. It was her big sister Penelope. She heard the tension in Mildred's voice and asked her what was wrong. Mildred, who had always confided in and looked up to Penelope, explained what had happened.

Penelope recommended that Mildred take some deep breaths and let out a big sigh each time she exhaled. After a few breaths, Mildred was feeling a little better and more relaxed. Sensing this, Penelope asked Mildred if she would like some advice. Mildred said she would, as this wasn't the first time this type of thing had happened when she was trying to help people.

Penelope said, "The fact that you recognize that there's a problem and want to make some changes so you won't feel so awful in the future is a fantastic insight." Hearing this made Mildred feel good.

Penelope then said, "It's a good quality that you want to help people solve their problems. However, it's always best to first ask them if they'd like to hear your opinion. If not, don't offer anything. And when you begin by using potentially threatening language, it can quickly create a problem. For example, even though I'm sure you didn't mean to be hurtful, when you began by telling your coworkers that they were wrong, they probably felt hurt and threatened. This probably made them tense—not a good situation if you want people to be open to your advice. In these kinds of situations, you might want to start by saying something more like 'Have you considered…' or 'How about…'"

Penelope then went on to say, "When people don't want to hear your solutions or disagree with them, it's best to back off. Don't get contentious, and know when to stop. If you continue to push it, then it's likely to turn into a situation like what you experienced with Sam and Penny: a stressful argument. At this point, you're working against your original intention: trying to help the other person. Instead, you're trying to demonstrate you're right and the other person is wrong, and by forcing the issue, you're trying to control their behavior. As a result, you may say things that are hurtful to others. Plus, the argument ends up hurting you, because you get really stressed. Does that make sense?"

Mildred sighed. Seeing the situation in this way, as Penelope described it, was painful. She felt ashamed, but she also recognized the truth in what Penelope was saying. After a pause, she said, "Yes, it does make sense. I don't feel great about it, but thanks to your insights and support, I know I can change my behavior. It may take a while, but I'm determined to succeed. I'll follow your advice and remember to take deep breaths and let out a big sigh when I'm starting to feel tense. Thank you so much."

The next day at work Mildred went up to Sam and Penelope and apologized for her behavior. She explained the situation to them and asked them for any assistance they could provide, especially if she reverted back to her problematic behavior. They both smiled and said they'd be happy to help. Sam then asked Mildred if she'd like to join them for lunch. A sense of warmth enveloped her, and she said, "I'd like that."

Practice   Identifying Unresolvable Problems

In this exercise, you'll reflect upon two things: unresolvable problems that you try to solve, and the people and events in your life that you try to control but cannot. On a blank page in your journal, make three columns. In the left-hand column, list the unresolvable problems you try to solve and the people and events you try to control but cannot. In the middle column, list the behaviors you engage in relative to those same two factors: trying to solve each of the unresolvable problems, and trying to control people and events that you cannot control. In the third column, list the feelings you experience as the result of each behavior. This kind of self-reflection is difficult. Take some time and be gentle with yourself. The point is not to criticize yourself, but to increase your awareness of your problematic behaviors and their costs.

Next, take some time to reflect upon what you've written in all three columns. Then look at the third column and focus on anything you've written that indicates stress, particularly unpleasant feelings such as anger, hostility, depression, anxiety, and tension. Recognize that the behavior that leads to these feelings is problematic because it doesn't work and also causes you stress. Then ask yourself why you continue to engage in behavior that doesn't work and that causes you stress.

The next step is to remove the behaviors associated with absolute beliefs that you must solve all the problems you perceive and that you can control people and events so they behave according to your expectations. Removing these behaviors may seem easier said than done. You're probably wondering how you can accomplish this.

You've already taken the first step by becoming aware of what these behaviors are. Next, you need to be attentive, bringing guan to the occurrence of these behaviors. When you see and feel that you're starting to engage in these behaviors, simply tell yourself to stop. Don't dwell on the behavior or the beliefs that spur it; instead, let out a big sigh. Sighing will change your focus and allow you to begin to relax. Take a few complete breaths to further support your change in focus and enhance your relaxation. Then withdraw from the situation and do something else.

Because you've probably been engaging in these behaviors for a long time, they may occur automatically. This is normal. However, it does mean that it will take some time to completely disrupt this automatic response. Again, this is normal. It's also an ongoing process. Throughout life, you will need to continue working on your thoughts, beliefs, and behaviors to simplify your life and to avoid chronic stress.

Interlude

Now let's turn to the physical approach to changing behavior in order to eliminate chronic stress. Before I cover the third postures in the Baduanjin and Yijinjing sequences, I'll introduce brisk walking. Should you need any reassurance that you're making progress, consider this: the simple fact that you're learning and practicing the qigong postures, and that you'll be adding brisk walking to your physical practices, indicates that you're making proactive changes in your behavior.

Practice   Walking Briskly

Research has clearly demonstrated that brisk walking is a beneficial form of moderate-intensity aerobic exercise (Harvard Health 2009). Although it has the same benefits as running, it doesn't have the detriments, such as the pounding of joints that can lead to injuries. When you're walking briskly, you should notice that your heart rate and breathing rate increase. These changes are normal and indicate that you're working at an aerobic level. In general, brisk walking is often defined as walking one mile in fifteen to twenty minutes or walking 120 to 135 steps a minute. Of course, this depends on your fitness level. If you haven't been exercising much, you'll want to begin with a slower pace.

To practice, make sure you have enough time available to walk for ten to thirty minutes. Find a place where you feel safe and where traffic, obstacles, and so on are minimal or nonexistent. You might try a park, around a track at a school, on the beach, or in your neighborhood. Before you begin, do a few simple stretching exercises, especially for your legs. Then, as you walk, make sure you are practicing guan and smiling. For your own safety, be aware of your environment.

If this is all new to you, start slowly, with just five minutes of brisk walking, and work up to twenty minutes. If you feel that you're in good shape, start with ten minutes of brisk walking and work up to thirty minutes. When you feel comfortable and fit at a particular duration, gradually increase the amount of time you're walking. You be the judge.

If time is a constraint, you can engage in several brisk ten-minute walking sessions during your day. Three brisk ten-minute walks spread throughout the day will be just as beneficial as one thirty-minute brisk walk. If you can, try to walk in the early morning, shortly after you get up. If this timing isn't feasible, late afternoon is fine. If neither works for you, find a time that does. Try to avoid walking when the sun is at its strongest, between 10 a.m. and 4 p.m.

Also avoid dehydration. Make sure you drink an adequate amount of water before and after your walk. You may want to carry a water bottle with you as you walk. To conclude each session, walk slowly for a few minutes to cool down. You may also want to do a few stretches after walking.

The first few times you engage in brisk walking, spend some time afterward reflecting upon what you felt and thought about while walking, and then write about this in your journal. What did you notice in your body? Your mind? Were you able to stay focused on walking briskly and practicing guan? Did you smile while walking? Did you find yourself making any negative judgments about walking? Did you find yourself wanting to quit? Also notice and write about what you feel and think after you finish the walk. You may wish to continue to write about this in your journal from time to time, even after you've established the practice.

Qigong

Now it's time to learn the third posture of the Baduanjin and Yijinjing sequences. First learn each new movement, then perform it in the sequence, starting with the first posture and continuing through the second posture and into the new one. As you practice, remember to apply guan, breathe naturally, and smile. Upon finishing each sequence with the new posture, reflect upon your experiences while performing it. What were your body and mind telling you about yourself? Take some time to write in your journal about what you experienced while performing these movements.

Practice Posture 3 of the Baduanjin Sequence: Beating the Heavenly Drum

Maintaining the Sitting in Stillness posture, which you returned to from the second posture, Gently Clicking Your Teeth and Embracing Kunlun Mountain, breathe naturally and once again lift your palms in front of your chest and rub them together until they feel warm. Then place your palms over your ears, with the tips of your middle fingers touching at the back of your head. Try to block out the sounds in your environment.

Next, place your index fingers on top of your middle fingers (left index finger on left middle finger, and right index finger on right middle finger). Then simply snap your right index finger straight down onto the back of your head. You should hear the sound of your finger striking your head. As you return it to resting on top of the right middle finger, snap down your left index finger. As you return it to resting on top of the left middle finger, snap down your right index finger. Essentially, you are simply alternating the strikes in a yin and yang format. As your fingers work together, one striking down while the other rises up, and moving back and forth (right, left, right, and so on), both take on the qualities of yin and yang.

Practice guan through these movements. Be aware of the feeling of your palms covering your ears and your fingers snapping down on the back of your head. Be aware of the sound that occurs when each finger makes contact with your head. Complete a total of nine repetitions, with one right strike and one left strike being one repetition. After completing the ninth repetition, let your hands return to their original position so that you are once again in the position Sitting in Stillness.

Beating the Heavenly Drum helps clear the mind. While clicking the teeth in the second posture moves from inside outward, the finger snaps in this third posture move from the outside inward. Both of these postures bring focus to the body, stilling and emptying the mind.

Practice Posture 3 of the Yijinjing Sequence: Holding a Ball in Front of Your Abdomen

From the second posture, Holding a Ball in Front of Your Chest, maintain the same hand, arm, and feet positions and, while breathing naturally, simply lower your arms until your hands are in line with your belly button or thereabouts. Continue to breathe naturally. Stay in this position for one to two minutes, smiling and practicing guan.

This posture continues to help you root and center yourself and clear your mind. It also helps you develop awareness of your body for the purpose of listening to what your body tells you about yourself when in a new position.

Conclusion

This chapter focused on simplifying your behaviors—another aspect of simplifying your life, which is one of the three components of the Taoist path. It explored eating, drinking, sleeping, and exercise behaviors and the damage caused by attempting to solve unresolvable problems and change that which you cannot change. The next chapter explores one of the most fundamental qualities across all forms of Taoism: *wuwei*, or noninterference.

The Taoist approach and the various techniques you've been learning and practicing may be quite new to you and perhaps quite challenging. I want to congratulate you for trying them and persevering. One of the most difficult barriers is overcoming resistance to simply taking the first step. At this point, you have traveled far beyond the first step.

Chapter 5

Not Interfering with Yourself or Others

Qingcheng Shan, outside of Chengdu in Sichuan, China, is a famous mountain that is home to many Taoist temples, and is believed to be the location where Taoism originated. On this mountain is a large wall with the following Chinese words engraved upon it in very large characters: *Da Dao Wuwei*, which translates as "The Great Tao Does Not Interfere."

"The Great Tao Does Not Interfere" refers to the observation that Tao is the basis for existence and allows existence to follow its own course. Tao doesn't interfere with the process. In Taoism, the natural noninterfering behavior of the sky and the earth, which simply behave, without any self-imposed barriers, is a guide for how to behave naturally in the world.

Wuwei, or noninterference, is the fundamental Taoist way of being, behaving, feeling, interacting, and thinking. Basically, it means not interfering, physically or psychologically, with ourselves or others. It means being neither excessive nor deficient in our thinking and behavior. Excessive or deficient thinking and behavior interfere with such basics as eating, drinking, sleeping, and exercise, and compromise not only the body but also the mind. Such thinking and behavior give rise to and maintain chronic stress. Therefore, wuwei essentially means engaging in life without being chronically stressed. According to the Taoist text the *Zhuangzi*, true happiness can only be found through wuwei (Guo 1974).

Tao, Wuwei, and Naturalness

As noted in chapter 1, Tao is dynamic empty space. Everything that occurs requires dynamic empty space. Be it eating, drinking, moving about, breathing, reproducing, talking, just sitting, or what have you, everything occupies, surrounds, or is surrounded by empty space. It is the natural process from which everything arises and transforms, and to which everything returns. As such, everything is interrelated and linked by Tao. As dynamic empty space, Tao allows all things to follow their natural course. It does not interfere.

Our problem is that we don't follow our natural course because we focus on forms or things, both tangible and intangible, and believe separation is what is natural. We don't realize that while form is beneficial, it is dynamic empty space that allows form to have a function. For example, the reason why a drinking glass (a form) is beneficial (holds liquids) is because of the empty space into which liquids are poured (function). As a result of our misunderstanding, we continually interfere with ourselves by piling up more and more stuff, physically and psychologically, compromising our view of what Taoists refer to as the natural behavior of existence. We are too full!

We make our life way too complex. Simple behaviors such as eating are almost always subject to interference from distractions: computers, TV, cell phones, reading material, radio, worrying, whining, and on and on. We no longer just eat. There is too much stuff in the way. Our eating is guided by artificiality, not naturalness. The consequences of these kinds of behavior lead us down the path to chronic stress.

The focus of early Taoist writers was on ziran, or naturalness, and simplifying life. In this context, naturalness means being neither excessive nor deficient in our thoughts and behavior. We don't interfere, physically or psychologically, with ourselves or others. As a result, our minds are still and empty of problematic thoughts, judgments, and beliefs. We simplify our lives by eliminating the clutter and barriers, both physical and psychological, that interfere with living in a manner free from chronic stress. It is an emptying out, so to speak.

This process of simplifying life is, essentially, a movement toward integration and living increasingly in harmony with dynamic empty space. The more barriers we eliminate, the more freedom we have to act naturally. So, in the example of eating, by eliminating all of the distractions that serve as barriers, we can eat in a natural, stress-free manner. We aren't interfering with ourselves as we eat. Our minds are still and empty. We eat from the position of wuwei—empty, natural, and in harmony with Tao.

In Taoism, this movement toward integration, naturalness, and dynamic empty space follows a natural progression that links the behavioral patterns of humans with the empty and noninterfering natural patterns of the earth, the sky, and Tao itself (Wang 1993). Thus, Taoism offers a model or guideline based on the natural behavior of the earth and sky that eliminates chronic stress and eventually, if this is your goal, leads to being in harmony with Tao.

The Path to Wuwei

The manner in which wuwei becomes the norm rather than the exception is a continual process of pruning, letting go, forgetting, and releasing artificiality, barriers, and hindrances. It is a process of emptying out— essentially simplifying life cognitively, emotionally, and behaviorally. As wuwei increasingly becomes the norm, we become increasingly natural in our behavior. We become more harmonious with the earth, the sky, and Tao.

Wuwei is initially developed by focused and direct practice, consciously directing our attention to the artificiality, barriers, and hindrances we need to eliminate from our lives so we can be free from chronic stress. We need to behaviorally remove them, be they physical or psychological. While this starts us on the road to wuwei, it is through the practice of meditation, both moving and still, that we fully develop wuwei and root it into our lives.

Not Interfering with Ourselves

Not interfering with ourselves means just that. It is eliminating beliefs, thoughts, judgments, and behaviors that activate and maintain the fight-or-flight response. All chronic, absolute, rigid, black-and-white thinking, including whining, complaining, criticizing, moaning, demeaning, and judging, is threat based and interferes with our physical and psychological functioning. This kind of thinking drives many behaviors that sabotage our health and well-being.

We each need to take an honest, nonjudgmental look at ourselves and ask, "What am I doing that compromises my own physical and psychological functioning? How am I getting in my own way?" Although there are many areas where we interfere with ourselves, in this chapter I'll focus on three specific areas where we often interfere with ourselves: eating and drinking, sleeping, and exercise.

Mark, Gary, and Damian's Story

Mark, Gary, and Damian were all in the same large psychology class at university. Mark was always focused in class and loved learning. Even though Gary tried to pay attention in class, he was anxious and spent a lot of energy doubting himself. Damian didn't pay much attention in class; instead, he usually played games on his smartphone.

A few days before their midterm exam, Mark and Gary decided to meet at the library to study. They invited Damian to join them, but he said he didn't think he needed any extra study time and preferred to hang out with his friends. Gary was anxious about the exam, and as he and Mark studied, he kept saying, "I'm not going to do well. This stuff is too hard. I can't do it." Mark tried to reassure Gary, telling him that he was smart and capable of learning the material. They studied together for a few hours and then parted ways.

For the next two days, Mark studied for about an hour or so each day. Mark was also in a religious studies class that had included a discussion of Taoism early on. He had appreciated the concept of wuwei, or not interfering with yourself, and had continued to do a simple breath-based meditation he'd learned in that class, practicing it each day for about ten minutes. In addition, he went out for a brisk walk each day for about thirty minutes. The day before the exam, he studied, meditated, went for his walk, and thought about wuwei. That night, he went to bed early.

Gary continued to worry about the exam and doubt himself. Each day, he spent four hours studying for the exam. The night before the exam, he stayed up half the night studying.

Damian continued to hang out with friends and play computer games. He hardly even looked at his psychology textbook. The night before the exam, he crammed for an hour. Figuring he'd put in enough time studying to pass the exam, he went out with some friends and stayed out late.

On the day of the exam, Mark felt at ease. Sitting in the classroom with his mind empty of distractions, he read the questions, smiled, and started to fill in his responses. Gary was tired and anxious, and his mind was full of negative judgments and doubt. He looked at the questions, told himself the test was really hard, and wondered if he could pass the exam. Damian was also tired, and as he looked at the questions, he realized he didn't have a clue about how to answer. He became extremely anxious, his mind cluttered and racing.

Not surprisingly, Mark aced the exam. He had approached it in a natural, holistic manner. Because his mind was empty of distractions and problematic thoughts, judgments, and beliefs, he didn't interfere with himself. His behavior in preparing for the test, including how he studied, was neither excessive nor deficient. He was free of chronic stress. His yin and yang were in harmony.

Gary barely passed. His mind was agitated, cluttered, and highly distractible. His thoughts, judgments, and beliefs were problematic. Gary interfered with himself by constantly worrying and doubting himself when he looked at the questions. His behavior in preparing for the test also interfered with his performance because he was excessive in his studying, was deficient in his sleep, and didn't recognize his chronic stress or do anything to address it. His yin and yang were not in harmony.

Damian failed. His mind was agitated and muddled, and he couldn't focus. His thoughts, judgments, and beliefs were problematic. Damian's behavior in preparing for the test interfered with his performance because he was deficient in his studying, deficient in his sleep, and excessive in having fun. In addition, he interfered with himself by getting highly anxious when he looked at the questions. His yin and yang were not in harmony.

Wuwei and Eating and Drinking

By not eating enough or eating too much, we interfere with our own well-being. By not drinking enough water or drinking too many unhealthful beverages, we interfere with our own well-being.

In chapter 2, I asked you to participate in the exercise Eating with Guan. Part of that exercise involved not engaging in any activities while eating. Essentially, you were asked to remove anything that interfered with focusing solely on eating. You were behaviorally participating in the process of wuwei.

Psychologically, when we eat we need to have our minds focused on just eating, not thinking about anything else. We certainly don't want any negative thoughts, such as worrying, complaining, criticizing, moaning, or whining, in our heads while we're eating. As you now know, all of these forms of thinking are threat based and can activate and maintain the fight-or-flight response. It's best if nothing interferes with eating, but stress is particularly problematic because it also interferes with digestion. When we remove these barriers, we are no longer interfering with ourselves. Psychologically, we are participating in wuwei as we eat.

For Taoists, eating is an occasion to slow down and enjoy a normal function of life. Moderation is key not only in what and how much we eat, but also in how we eat. Most people tend to eat too quickly, which interferes with the natural functioning of the body. We aren't wired to shovel food down our throats in a matter of seconds. We need to taste and thoroughly chew our food before swallowing. We need to take our time and eat in a natural, stress-free manner.

Practice   Reflecting on Wuwei with Eating and Drinking

Take some time to think about how you interfere with your own eating and drinking. Consider meals, snacks, and various beverages that you drink throughout the day. This includes when you're eating with others. Is there anything that you do or anything about the context in which you eat that interferes with just eating and drinking? Make a list of anything that interferes with your eating and drinking in your journal and reflect upon it. What can you remove from this list?

Next, slowly start practicing wuwei by eliminating just one or two things that interfere with your eating and drinking. After you do so, come back to your journal and note what you notice about your experience of eating and drinking after removing these things. This is a gradual process, so start small and remove more as you feel more comfortable with the approach. You can try this with just one meal or snack or even just part of a meal. The bottom line is that when you have a meal, it's best to slow down and simply focus on eating and drinking. This will help prevent stress.

Wuwei and Sleeping

While there are many external factors that can interfere with getting enough sleep, one of the main causes of insomnia and other sleep problems is stress created by our own thinking and behavior (Colbert 2006). We are interfering with ourselves. We need to learn how to stop interfering with ourselves. We need to practice wuwei.

Susan's Story

Susan, a single woman in her late thirties who worked in a crowded office, was prone to anxiety. Most nights after getting in bed, she would lie awake obsessing about her social interactions that day, fearing that she had alienated people, and worrying about what might happen the next day. This left her so stressed that she couldn't get to sleep. About an hour or so into her nightly rumination, she would think about how late it was and worry about not getting to sleep. After another hour or so, she usually passed out—often only to wake up suddenly in the middle of the night. Then she worried about waking up, and it usually took another thirty minutes or so for her get to back to sleep.

Most mornings Susan was extremely tired. She frequently had headaches and had a hard time focusing. She drank a lot of coffee—often an entire pot each morning—until she felt some sense of being alert. This had been going on for some time, and it was affecting both her health and her performance at work. Although she had tried over-the-counter sleep medications, they left her feeling foggy and out of sorts. Besides, she didn't want to become dependent on them. The last straw came when her boss called her in to his office to complain about Susan's last assignment, which she'd turned in late and in terrible shape. He wanted to know what was wrong. In that meeting, Susan finally reached the point where she knew she needed to do something different to try to improve her sleep, but she wasn't sure what.

Susan's usual route for walking home from work took her past a building where taijiquan classes were taught. She had heard a bit about taijiquan, and although she was skeptical, she wondered if it might help. She did some research and found an article in the journal *Sleep*. Its conclusion was that taijiquan was helpful in improving sleep. So one day on her way home from work, she stopped in and talked with one of the instructors. She explained her problem and then asked whether taijiquan might help with her sleep. The instructor smiled and said, "It can definitely help. From what you describe, it's clear that you're thinking while you're lying in bed, and this is cluttering your mind, stressing you out, and interfering with getting to sleep. You need to learn how to empty out your mind. In fact, right now, at no charge, I can teach you a simple meditative technique that will help you empty your mind and get to sleep."

Susan said she'd love to hear it, so the instructor told her, "When you get into bed, make sure all the lights are off, then simply focus on following your breath and think of nothing else. Focus on just inhaling slowly and deeply, and then exhaling slowly and deeply. As you inhale, let your abdomen naturally expand, and as you inhale, let it contract naturally." He demonstrated this breathing technique and asked Susan to give it a try so he could make sure she was doing it correctly.

He went on to say, "If you find yourself becoming distracted by anything, such as sounds or your thoughts and worries, this is normal. Don't dwell on these distractions or make any judgments about them, or about yourself for having them. Just refocus on following your breath. Practice this technique every night when you go to bed. It will take a while to develop your focus and see benefits. The key is to practice!"

Within a week Susan was falling asleep much more quickly and wasn't waking up in the middle of the night. Her headaches were gone, her focus was much improved, and she felt energized. She was no longer interfering with herself in regard to sleep. Impressed with these results, she decided to start taking taijiquan classes to see what other benefits she might experience.

Wuwei and Exercise

Our bodies are wired for motion. While being active on a regular basis was the norm for our distant ancestors, it isn't the case for most people in affluent societies today. We have all kinds of machines that move us about, such as cars, trains, and buses, and endless other machines to distract us and keep us from moving about, such as cell phones, TVs, and computers. As a result, we live a sedentary lifestyle that's detrimental to our health and well-being—something the obesity problem in this country amply demonstrates.

We need to exercise. Doing so is indisputably beneficial for our physical and psychological health. It also helps us eliminate chronic stress. The evidence in favor of exercising is overwhelming.

Unfortunately, most of us tend to interfere, physically and psychologically, with our natural need to exercise. One of the primary ways we interfere with ourselves is by making excuses why we can't exercise (Waehner 2012), such as "I'm too tired," "It's too complicated," "I don't have enough time," "It's too hard," "It hurts," "I don't like to sweat," "I don't feel like it," "It's too much of a commitment," "I can't do it on a regular and consistent basis," "I can't stay motivated," "It's too expensive," "I don't know how," and "Changes aren't occurring quickly enough." Most likely, these are generated from underlying absolute, threat-based beliefs and judgments about exercise.

In the Taoist approach, when we exercise, we need to be focusing solely on exercising. Our minds need to be empty of distractions. If we whine, complain, have hostile thoughts, and so on while exercising, we're interfering with ourselves and stressing ourselves out. We can't receive much benefit from exercise if we're stressed while engaging in it.

If you currently aren't exercising, you may wonder how to get started. First, remember that the past is gone. Everything that you've previously done and experienced in regard to exercise is over. Let it go. Forget about it and stop judging yourself about what has happened or what you're afraid will happen. Practice wuwei and guan.

Not Interfering with Others

The second aspect of wuwei is not interfering with others. In this context, wuwei means not trying to manipulate, control, or force other people to do what you want for your own benefit. It means not trying to coerce other people to agree with your opinions, your worldview, your political perspectives, your values, or how you think people ought to behave. Practicing wuwei while interacting with others means not yelling, demeaning, belittling, criticizing, or judging them.

Do you remember Mildred's story, in chapter 3? Her behavior with her coworkers, Sam and Penny, is a prime example of not practicing wuwei. It was also symptomatic of how Mildred lived her life, constantly interfering with herself and others. All the advice her sister Penelope offered basically encouraged Mildred to practice wuwei. Given everything you've learned in this chapter, you might wish to reread that story to see if you have new insight about the practice of wuwei.

Not interfering with others means listening to them, exchanging ideas, and providing constructive criticism when warranted. It means positively supporting and facilitating others as they naturally work out their destiny. It means creating an environment where your interactions with others are conducive to growth and well-being.

Practice   Reflecting on Wuwei with Others

Take a moment to reflect upon recent interactions with other people that felt stressful. Write about a few of these interactions in your journal. What was going on in those situations? Did you sincerely listen to the other person? Did you find yourself interfering with others in some manner? Were you trying to convince others that you were right and they were wrong? Was the interaction contentious? What do you need to eliminate or stop doing to prevent these kinds of interactions in the future?

Practice   Extending Wuwei to Yourself

This exercise (adapted from Santee 2007) asks you to make a conscious effort to practice wuwei with yourself. Pick a day to focus on practicing wuwei with yourself. Remember, wuwei means not interfering with yourself—getting out of your own way and not ruminating, complaining, or whining. This practice will help you eliminate self-imposed criticisms, restrictions, barriers, guilt, and doubt, which prevent you from moving forward and experiencing positive growth.

On the day you've chosen, throughout the day remember to observe yourself, your thoughts, and your actions. Is your mind cluttered with negative barriers? What triggers the negativity? Does it arise due to certain events or situations, or is it just habit or your general worldview? How do you interfere with yourself, and how often? How do you feel when you interfere with yourself? You might wish to write about all of this in your journal.

To practice wuwei with yourself, stay in the present and be nonjudgmental. This will require conscious effort. It will be challenging and will take time and practice to develop. Negativity, doubts, and self-criticisms will continue to arise. You've been practicing these negative thinking patterns for years, and they're well conditioned. However, they can only endure if you hold on to them with your judgments and thoughts. See what negativity and barriers you can eliminate. If you remain in the present and are nonjudgmental, the negativity and limitations will fade away. They only persist if you feed them with judgments.

After practicing wuwei with yourself, reflect on how you feel. What do you experience? Compare this to your experience when you don't practice wuwei with yourself. What do you notice? Spend some time writing about your experiences and the differences between them in your journal.

Interlude

The first part of this chapter discussed wuwei, ziran, and emptiness from a mental perspective and explored ways to develop these qualities. The remainder of the chapter turns to the physical component: qigong postures that will help you experience and develop wuwei, ziran, and emptiness.

Qigong

When practicing the qigong postures, it's important that you not interfere with yourself while performing them. If you find yourself getting distracted, don't dwell on those distractions or make any judgments about them or about yourself for having them; just refocus on your breathing and continue with the movements. This will train your mind to be empty, much like the empty space of Tao.

As always, first practice the preceding postures in the sequence, then add the new posture. Regarding your qigong practice, don't be deficient or excessive. Not doing enough won't help your chronic stress. Doing too much will just create more stress. This approach embodies wuwei, or noninterference. The easing of chronic stress as you practice wuwei is naturalness, or ziran.

Upon finishing each sequence with the new posture, reflect upon your experiences while performing it. What were your body and mind telling you about yourself? Take some time to write in your journal about what you experienced while performing these movements.

Practice   Posture 4 of the Baduanjin Sequence: Pushing the Mountain

Pushing the Mountain strengthens your core, stretches your back and arms, and loosens your neck. From the Sitting in Stillness posture, which you returned to after Beating the Heavenly Drum, take a deep breath and bring your hands toward the center of your abdomen with your palms facing up and your fingertips touching. Pull your hands upward, palms still facing up and fingertips continuing to touch, until they are at the level of your chest (at nipple level). Exhale.

Take a deep breath. As you exhale, rotate your hands inward so that your palms face first your chest, then downward, then outward, in one continuous movement, ending with your palms facing away from your body. At the same time, slowly turn your torso and neck to the left and push your hands forward, away from your body. You should be looking over your left shoulder.

Next, as you inhale deeply, slowly turn your torso and neck back to center while rotating your palms downward and inward and simultaneously bringing them back toward your body, returning them to earlier position: palms facing up and fingertips touching at nipple level. You should now be facing forward.

Repeat the same process on the right side: Rotate your palms inward, down, and then out and push your hands forward while exhaling and turning and looking over your right shoulder. Then inhale and return to center as you rotate your palms down, inward, and then upward while pulling your hands in toward your body. Completing both sides is one repetition. Repeat this process eight more times, for a total of nine repetitions. Remember to practice guan and smile throughout. To finish, stretch out your legs and stand up.

Practice   Posture 4 of the Yijinjing Sequence: Holding a Staff Across Your Chest

Holding a Staff Across Your Chest (here adapted from Santee 2011) releases tension in the hands, arms, upper back, and shoulders by stretching these areas. It also helps loosen the shoulder joints. After completing the previous posture, Holding a Ball in Front of Your Abdomen, take a deep breath. As you exhale, rotate your palms so they face upward and let your arms arc out to the sides while also raising them to shoulder level. Your elbows should remain slightly bent. Extend your fingertips outward while twisting your hands and arms to the rear, like a screw being screwed into a wall. The tension in your arms should be quite apparent. Visualize a heavy staff running across your chest from your left palm to your right palm. The staff is being supported and pushed up by your palms. The overall sensation should be feeling your arms moving in three directions—up, to the side, and to the rear—at the same time. Using guan, focus your mind on the center of your palms. Breathe naturally. Maintain this posture for one to two minutes.

Next, exhale and let your arms uncoil. Following the same arc in reverse, simply let your arms float down and return to the posture Holding a Ball in Front of Your Abdomen. You should have a distinct sense of an inward twisting of both your arms and your hands toward the center of the imaginary ball that you're holding. Continue to breathe naturally. Hold this position for one to two minutes. Then let your arms return to your sides and resume the Wuji Standing posture.

Conclusion

Practicing wuwei can be a challenge and, at times, frustrating. Remember that you're trying to eliminate problematic physical and psychological behaviors that you've been engaging in for years. Be patient. Allow the awareness that these behaviors lead to chronic stress to motivate you to practice wuwei daily. Having read this far and dedicated yourself to practicing the various exercises and techniques in this book, you are well on the road to finding calm and balance and simplifying your life.

Part 3

Reducing Your Desires

Chapter 6

Understanding Desires

From the time we get up in the morning until the time we go to bed at night, we are vulnerable to an onslaught of advertisements across all types of media telling us what we should desire and obtain in order to be happy, feel good about ourselves, and be accepted by others. In addition, friends, family members, acquaintances, colleagues, coworkers, and others often tell us what we should desire, get, see, or watch, where and what we should eat, and so on in order for their desires—yes, *their* desires—to be met.

In a very real sense, and unfortunately, our self-worth often hinges on attaining what others tell us we should desire. If we don't please them, we fear that they may not like or appreciate us. This is clearly a threat to our self-worth and leads to chronic stress.

If we haven't attained the things that others say we should desire, we feel threatened and stressed until we obtain them. If we do attain these things, we still feel threatened because we're afraid we'll lose them or because we think they aren't enough. As a result, we are still chronically stressed. This becomes an ongoing cycle in which we are never satisfied.

We all have basic desires that are part of our evolutionary tool kit, such as for safety, security, shelter, food, a good income, companionship, sex, having children, being healthy, getting adequate movement or exercise, feeling good, being happy, and being liked. All of these have an impact on how we think, feel, and behave. They are also natural.

In addition, we have desires driven by social expectations, such as for fame, status, wealth, power, longevity, or always looking good or being youthful. These also have an impact on how we think, feel, and behave and are not inherently problematic.

However, when any of our desires, whether basic or socially driven, are continually excessive or deficient and lead to chronic stress, they become problematic. They cannot be satisfied. We don't know when enough is enough or how to stop indulging in or pursuing these desires. The end result is the physical and psychological harm of chronic stress.

When traveling the Taoist path to removing chronic stress, it is important to remember that desires, thoughts, beliefs, judgments, feelings, behavior, and environment are all intimately intertwined and interrelated. All have a bearing on your center and root and the free and natural flow of qi. When they are neither excessive nor deficient, your yin and yang are in harmony not only within yourself, but also with the environment around you.

Taoism and Desires

Across Taoist history and in numerous Taoist texts, excessive or deficient desires are viewed as a fundamental cause of fragmentation and separation from Tao. Excessive or deficient desires result in disaster, misfortune, danger, vulnerability, illness, and tragedy. Excessive or deficient desires disrupt and agitate both the mind and the body. Because of our excessive or deficient desires, we are selfish, self-centered, and chronically stressed. In fact, these problematic desires prevent us from being free from chronic stress.

While our basic desires can certainly become excessive or deficient, Taoist teachings tend to focus on excessive socially driven desires, which tend to compromise basic desires, such as eating, drinking, sleeping, and exercise, and therefore contribute to chronic stress. In Taoism, the senses and the mind are seen as the primary vehicles for excessive or deficient desires. Regarding excessive desires, our senses and mind pull us out of ourselves and toward various objects in our environment that our society has determined to be of importance for self-worth. As a result, we ignore our own health and well-being as we continually seek what society has deemed to be valuable and important. This divide between our own health and well-being and the values and desires created by society has long been a significant concern within Taoism.

Is attaining fame or excessive wealth worth losing your health and well-being? Is it worth being chronically stressed? The problem is that we don't know when enough is enough. We don't know when to stop. Our desires become excessive because we are continually bombarded with messages about how we should look and what we should possess, eat, drink, wear, and do so we can feel good about ourselves. This bombardment never ends, no matter how much or what we attain, as society continues to create more and more new things we need to have or be—or ways we shouldn't be, as in the cultural message that women must be deficient in weight in order to be beautiful. As a result, we can never be satisfied. Our desires become excessive.

Desires and Time

A major source of chronic stress for many people is the perception that they simply don't have enough time to accomplish all the tasks they think they need to complete. Yet many of these tasks are directly linked to excessive desires.

The more desires we have, the more time we spend trying to satisfy them. The time we waste thinking about and trying to satisfy our excessive desires, and the time we spend complaining about what we don't have, significantly contribute to our lack of time. This is time we can never get back. And because excessive desires can never be satisfied, we will never have enough time. As a result, we become more and more impatient, which feeds chronic stress.

From the Taoist perspective, if we want to eliminate our impatience, gain control of our time, and free ourselves from chronic stress, we need to remove not only our excessive desires, but also our deficient desires. More generally, we need to reduce our desires overall in order to simplify our lives.

Desires and Sleep

Chapter 4 looked at how mental behaviors, such as worrying and obsessing at bedtime, create problems with getting to sleep, staying asleep, and sleeping restfully. Chapter 5 discussed how practicing wuwei, or noninterference, can assist us in getting to sleep, staying asleep, and sleeping restfully. Here, I'll take a brief look at how desires disrupt sleep.

From the Taoist perspective, excessive desires, including unfulfilled desires, hopes, and wishful thinking, disturb both the mind and the body. They give rise to and maintain chronic stress. If at bedtime we habitually worry and ruminate about what we don't have but desire, what we wish would happen, what we want to get rid of, and what we hope won't happen, our minds will be agitated, making it difficult to fall asleep, stay asleep, and sleep restfully. Not getting enough restful sleep further stresses the body and mind, adding to our chronic stress. Our excessive desires so overwhelm us that they outweigh our natural desire for sleep. Essentially, our desire for sleep is deficient. In this situation, both excessive and deficient desires interfere with sleep and lead to chronic stress, harming us physically and psychologically.

The teachings of Taoism indicate that at bedtime we should be free of deliberations, expectations, emotions, and desires. This allows the mind to be still, empty, and anchored in a quiet place, which promotes deep, dreamless, undisturbed, restful, and adequate sleep (Guo 1974).

Desires and Eating

There is no question that certain foods taste good. They taste good because evolution has taught us to eat them to get the energy we need to engage life. If we didn't have the desire to eat, we wouldn't have the energy to sustain life. We would simply die.

The foods that tend to taste so good primarily contain sugar and fat. In addition to providing the energy we need for life, they tend to make us feel better emotionally. Therefore, we call them comfort foods. For about 40 percent of people, stress increases the desire for these foods (Dallman 2009). By making us feel better, they temporarily reduce the negative symptoms of stress. In this way, the desire for comfort foods in response to stress is reinforced. When stress becomes chronic, the desire for these comfort foods becomes excessive. People start taking in far more calories than they need and become overweight or obese (Harvard Health 2012). The additional weight adds another stressor that compromises their well-being.

For another 40 percent of people, stress results in a reduction in the desire to eat (Dallman 2009). When such people experience chronic stress, their desire to eat becomes deficient, resulting in unhealthful weight loss. This too is detrimental to well-being.

In order to eliminate the excessive or deficient desires that interfere with eating, we need to manage our stress and also focus on specific eating habits. In chapter 2, you learned the practice of Eating with Guan. In chapter 5, you learned about not interfering with yourself (wuwei) in regard to eating. The integrated Taoist approach calls for eating a balanced diet, eating moderately, not interfering with yourself in regard to eating, and being present while eating.

Desires and Exercise

In the United States and other countries with large numbers of overweight and obese people, the problem is compounded by a generally deficient desire for exercise. Although our bodies are wired for motion, our society generally reinforces activities that require and reinforce a sedentary lifestyle, such as eating, drinking, texting, surfing the Web, watching TV, social networking, and playing video games. Given these many distractions, people tend to come up with numerous excuses for not exercising, as noted in chapter 5. In such cases, the desire to exercise is clearly deficient and contributes to chronic stress, which compromises well-being.

On the other hand, some people have an excessive desire to exercise. By overexercising, they chronically stress both mind and body and thereby put their health and well-being in jeopardy. Sometimes this happens because people overtrain in a quest to be the best. In other cases it occurs because people believe themselves to be fat; and, in a quest to be extremely thin, they manifest an excessive desire to exercise and a deficient desire to eat.

In all cases, we need to be aware of how excessive or deficient desires in regard to exercise interfere with our well-being and stress both mind and body. Once again, moderation is the key. Our yin and yang need to be in harmony.

Moderation, wuwei, and guan are all extremely helpful because they allow us to customize our lives to what is natural for each of us individually. As discussed in the previous chapter, we need to get out of our own way, stop being judgmental, and simply begin to exercise.

Practice Exploring and Reducing Your Desires

This exercise will help you explore your problematic desires—those that cause you to lose your center and root and result in your yin and yang being out of harmony. These are desires that are either excessive (too yang) or deficient (too yin) and that give rise to, maintain, or result from chronic stress. Continually eating too much is an excessive desire that results in weight gain, which chronically stresses the normal functioning of the body. Continually not eating enough is a deficient desire that results in weight loss, which also chronically stresses the normal functioning of the body. By becoming aware of these problematic desires and examining, moderating, or eliminating them, you can simplify your life, find your center and root, harmonize your yin and yang, and ease chronic stress.

For this exercise, you'll need to use your journal, a piece of paper, or a computer. Make two columns. Title one column "Excessive Desires," and the other "Deficient Desires." Then list all the desires that apply to you, placing each in the appropriate column. Be honest with yourself, and be specific. Here's an example.

Excessive Desires	Deficient Desires
Eating junk food	*Exercising*
Texting	*Drinking water*
Gaming	*Eating fruit*
Drinking alcohol	*Eating vegetables*
Sleeping	

This is the first step: becoming aware of your problematic desires. The next step is to examine each desire individually. Separately, list each problematic desire and give yourself space to answer the following questions for each one:

1. What do you get from this excessive or deficient desire?

2. What function does this desire perform for you?

3. Is it beneficial to your health? If not, why not?

4. Is it detrimental to your health? If so, how?

5. Can you avoid or change the environment in which this desire arises or is deficient? If so, how?

Be sure to actually write down your answers to these questions for each desire. If you are to reduce your chronic stress, it's crucial that you have a crystal-clear understanding of the problematic desires associated with your chronic stress.

While this type of inquiry is generally straightforward for excessive desires, it may seem tricky or confusing in regard to deficient desires. So let's take drinking water as an example. Most of us don't drink enough water and are unaware of how this can chronically stress the body and how it is linked to a wide variety of physical and psychological symptoms. Here's an example of how someone might answer the preceding questions for a deficient desire to drink water:

1. What do you get from this excessive or deficient desire? *Because water has no flavor and I don't feel I get anything from it, I don't have to drink much if any water.*

2. What function does this desire perform for you? *It allows me to drink something that I enjoy tasting instead, such as coffee, which gives me an energy boost and makes me feel good.*

3. Is it beneficial to your health? If not, why not? *Truthfully, no. If I don't get an adequate amount of water each day, my normal body functioning is compromised.*

4. Is it detrimental to your health? If so, how? *Yes. I experience a wide range of symptoms, such as problems with pain, energy, digestion, blood pressure, anxiety, constipation, diarrhea, memory problems, being easily distracted, and being*

confused and unable to focus, because of not drinking enough water.

5. Can you avoid or change the environment in which this desire arises or is deficient? If so, how? *No. I need to drink an adequate amount of water wherever I am.*

Having become aware of and examined these problematic excessive or deficient desires, the next step is to moderate or eliminate them. Excessive desires need to be decreased, while deficient desires need to be increased. This process of increasing and decreasing helps us establish our center and root and allows mind, body, and the environment to be in harmony.

The challenge, of course, is transferring this from an exercise on paper to and actual reduction or elimination of these excessive or deficient desires. Just remember to be moderate in your approach! Start with one of the problematic desires you explored above, for which your answers indicated that it is indeed stress producing and harmful to your well-being. Ask yourself what thinking and behavior you need to change in order to moderate or eliminate this desire. Once you've figured this out, just do it.

I'll use a deficient desire in regard to exercising as an example. If you believe that exercise is good for you and not exercising is bad for you, the next step is to change your behavior. Because the goal is to eliminate your chronic stress, your motivation to change your behavior is strong. Therefore, the first step of changing your behavior and actually exercising won't be a problem. Start with something simple and easy. If you already walk, brisk walking would be an excellent exercise to begin with. For example, you might start with a ten-minute or half-mile walk and gradually (not excessively) increase your time and distance until you are briskly walking two miles in thirty minutes. There is no rush to do more right away! The benefits you receive from brisk walking will reinforce your desire to continue doing this exercise and your behavioral commitment to doing it.

Interlude

The first part of this chapter discussed the mental approach to addressing and eliminating excessive and deficient desires associated with chronic stress. Now we'll turn to the physical approach. Remember, the Taoist path incorporates both a mental approach and a physical approach in establishing a harmonious relationship between mind, body, and environment. This harmonious relationship is centered and rooted between excessiveness and deficiency.

Qigong

In addition to learning the fifth postures of both the Baduanjin and the Yijinjing sequences, in this section you'll learn the Taoist meditative process of chanting while walking in a circle, created by Qiu Changqun about eight hundred years ago (Miller 1993; Santee 2009). With this technique, you not only exercise your body as you walk, but also train your attention and concentration. This meditative tool helps you still your mind and empty it of problematic desires, thoughts, beliefs, and judgments and the agitation and chronic stress they create.

As usual, upon finishing each of the Baduanjin and Yijinjing sequences with the new posture, reflect upon your experiences. What were your body and mind telling you about yourself? Take some time to write in your journal about what you experienced while performing these movements.

Practice   Circle Walking

As you now know, in Taoism, everything changes and transforms in a cyclic or circular process. The circle is fundamental to our lives, as is evident in the cyclic, intertwining, reciprocal relationship of yin and yang, the earth circling the sun, the moon circling the earth, the cycle of the four seasons, the blood circulating through the body, and even the electrons circling the nucleus of an atom. The Taoist circle-walking practice puts us in harmony with the circular motions of the universe at both the macro and micro levels. It accomplishes this by rooting and centering us in empty space in the context of the circle, allowing the energies of yin and yang to intermingle and flow freely and naturally.

By continually chanting or repeating a word or short phrase to yourself as you walk the circle, you train your mind to attend and concentrate, while also emptying it of the problematic desires that contribute to its agitation. This process will assist you in removing chronic stress as it creates a harmonious integrative relationship between mind, body, and environment.

To practice, find an area, inside or outside, where you can walk in a circle. Depending on where you'll walk, select either a small circle (eight total steps) or a medium circle (sixteen total steps). Walk around something, such as a tree or an object on the ground, perhaps a water bottle or a potted plant. This will help keep you focused and help keep the size of your circle consistent.

Select a word or short phrase that you can continually chant or quietly say to yourself with each step as you walk the circle. Make sure the word or phrase you choose is meaningful to you. It can be a positive affirmation, something from your philosophy of life, or related to your religious or spiritual tradition. Here are some examples: "Peace," "Love," "Happiness," "Wuwei," "Simplify," "Empty," "God," "I am free," "I am healthy," "I love my family," "I am energized," or "May everyone be safe."

Before beginning to walk, do some simple stretching to loosen up. Remember to practice guan and smile at all times. Then, breathing naturally, come into the Wuji Standing posture. As you stand, gently twist your torso to the left, toward the center of the circle, and look at the center of the circle at eye level. Begin walking the circle in a counterclockwise direction, starting with your left foot, using your natural gait, and keeping your gaze directed toward the center at eye level. A natural gait is placing your heel down first, followed by the rest of your foot and ending with your toes while pushing off with the back foot. Remember to continually repeat your word or phrase as you walk. Walk in a counterclockwise direction for thirty repetitions.

Next, simply turn around, gently twist your torso to the right, toward the center of the circle, and begin walking in a clockwise direction, starting with your right foot and keeping your gaze directed toward the center of the circle at eye level. Once you've completed thirty clockwise circles, walk in a noncircular manner for a few moments to cool down. Then drink some water.

To keep track of your repetitions, count them every time you complete a full circle. If you find yourself getting frustrated or distracted while walking, simply refocus on your word or phrase. If you lose count, begin again from ten.

As you feel more comfortable walking the circle, you can increase your speed, add more repetitions in both directions, or do both. It is probably most effective to do this practice about three times per week, taking a day off between sessions.

When you finish your first practice of the circle walk, reflect upon how you feel. What do you notice? Do you have any desires, or is your mind fairly empty and still? Recall how you felt while walking the circle. What did you notice? Did you have any desires (to do something else) or thoughts (such as *This is stupid*) or experience other distractions that interfered with your focus on walking? If so, what were they? What did you learn about yourself? Take some time to write about your experience in your journal.

Practice Posture 5 of the Baduanjin Sequence: Swishing Saliva in Your Mouth Thirty-Six Times

From the Sitting in Stillness posture, which you returned to after Pushing the Mountain, take a deep breath and let it out slowly. Look forward with your lips gently closed. Place your thumbs in your palms and lightly close your fingers around them, resting your fists on your lap or thighs. Breathe naturally.

Raise your fists upward, turning your palms to face forward (away from you), and contract your shoulder blades, which will bring your arms back and in line with your shoulders. Your upper arms should be aligned with your shoulders, with your elbows bent at right angles and your palms still facing forward. This movement stretches your upper back, chest, and shoulders.

Rotate your tongue across your outer gums in a counterclockwise direction thirty-six times. Then repeat this motion in the opposite direction. Next, move your tongue all around in your mouth. Finally, puff up your cheeks from side to side and also puff out the area behind your lips. At this point you should be well aware of the saliva in your mouth. Swish it all around your mouth. Then swallow it in three noisy gulps. Visualize it entering your lower dantian.

After the third swallow, slowly lower your fists to your thighs or lap, open them up with your palms facing each other, and return to the position Sitting in Stillness. Smile. Smiling naturally is an expression of a centered, rooted, and happy spirit, or *shen*. At this point, stretch out your legs, take a few breaths, and get up.

The Taoist practice of rotating and moving your tongue in your mouth and puffing out your cheeks and lips is a way to gather qi (vital energy, or breath) and mix it with the *jing*, or life essence, in your saliva (Robinet 1993). This mixture has both transforming qualities (qi) and nourishing qualities (jing). Swallowing the mixture and visualizing it entering your lower dantian combines it with the heat of the dantian and spreads it throughout the body, reducing or eliminating problems caused by stress (Kohn 2008a). In addition, visualizing the saliva mixture entering your lower dantian is believed to be helpful for developing one's center and stilling the mind. On a more mundane level, swallowing the saliva mixture is believed to aid digestion.

Practice Posture 5 of the Yijinjing Sequence: Supporting a Staff Above Your Head

To link the new movement, Supporting a Staff Above Your Head (adapted from Santee 2011), to the ending of the previous movement, Holding a Staff Across Your Chest, don't bring your hands back to your sides to the Wuji Standing posture; instead, stay in the posture Holding a Ball in Front of Your Abdomen. After a minute or two of breathing naturally in that position, take a deep breath.

As you exhale, bring your hands inward toward your belly button, stopping about a fist-width from your belly button with your palms facing up and your fingertips still pointing toward each other. Take another deep breath. As you exhale, lift your hands up with your palms still facing upward. When your hands reach the level of your eyes, keep your fingertips pointing toward each other and, in a continuous motion, rotate your hands inward, so that your palms face down; then outward, so that your palms face forward, away from you; then upward. Continue the motion, pushing your hands upward until your arms are almost fully extended but without locking your elbows. Your palms should be over your head facing up, and your fingertips should still be pointing toward each other.

At this point, rotate the thumb side of your hands inward until your fingers face backward over the top of your head. Extend your fingers toward the rear while pushing your palms upward and slightly twisting them inward. Visualize a heavy staff resting across your palms with the ends of the staff pointing to the sides. Your entire body should now be feeling the dynamic tension and twisting created by this form. The overall feeling in your arms and hands should be a sensation of moving in three directions—up, inward, and to the rear—at the same time. Focus on the center of your palms. You should feel your chest and abdominal cavity opening up and a stretching in your hamstrings and calves. Your entire body is being stretched. Your muscles are tense. Continue breathing deeply and naturally. Hold this position for one to two minutes.

When you're ready to finish this position, take a deep breath. As you exhale, relax and push your hands out to the sides, your palms facing outward, and allow them to circle downward until they return to the position Holding a Ball in Front of Your Abdomen. You should have a distinct sense of an inward twisting of both your arms and your hands toward the center of the imaginary ball that you're holding. Your palms should be facing inward and slightly upward. Focus your mind on a point about three inches below your belly button (your lower dantian). Breathe naturally and hold this position for one to two minutes. Then let your arms return to your sides and resume the Wuji Standing posture.

Remember, for this movement and for all the Yijinjing movements discussed thus far, your eyes are open and looking forward. Your mouth is closed, with your teeth gently touching each other. Your head is pulled up, like a puppet on string, gently stretching your neck.

This movement releases tension in your hands, arms, shoulders, and legs. It also opens up and relieves tension in your neck, chest, back, and abdominal cavity. It essentially allows your entire body—neck, arms, legs, shoulders, back, chest, and abdomen—to stretch at the same time.

Conclusion

This chapter focused on how excessive or deficient desires lead to chronic stress and compromise the natural functioning of mind and body. This is especially the case in regard to sleeping, eating, and exercise. You learned several exercises and practices that can assist you in eliminating these problematic desires and the chronic stress associated with them. The next chapter looks at how we get entangled in the affairs of the world and how this entanglement leads to chronic stress.

But before you read on, take a deep breath, smile, and congratulate yourself for continuing on the Taoist path to relieving your chronic stress. Are you beginning to see and feel yourself becoming more calm and balanced? Do you notice that you're simplifying your life? Remember, the key is to practice!

Chapter 7

Not Getting Entangled in the Activities of the World

This chapter looks at how chronic stress may be related to and controlled by our interactions with the various activities that make up our world. To what extent do our activities in the world, such as working, socializing, pursuing recreation, and volunteering, lead to and maintain our chronic stress? While each of these areas may be, in and of itself, important for our overall health and well-being, excessive involvement with any of them can put us out of balance. And in addition to these more basic activities, in the modern world we have endless options to interact with the world through technology, such as through texting, tweeting, blogging, and using the Internet. Becoming entangled with these activities also puts us out of balance. We become chronically stressed, compromising our physical, psychological, interpersonal, and occupational functioning.

Entanglement in the activities of the world can be so insidious that we don't even recognize it as a potential source of chronic stress. How can socializing, helping others, volunteering, and so on possibly be a source of chronic stress? To a large degree, these activities become stressful because we don't recognize how excessive involvement in them eats up our time—time that we need to devote to other areas of our lives if we are to be in balance and healthy. When we believe that what we're doing is good and beneficial for others, we may sacrifice our time and remain blind to how this entanglement is harming us and may also be harming others.

In addition, when we cannot engage in the activities we're entangled with, we often appear to go through withdrawal. Once again, we are out of balance. We may become irritated, angry, distractible, hyperactive, anxious, depressed, unable to focus, and so on. Our thinking may be compromised. We may have physical symptoms such as headaches or stomachaches. Our sleep and eating may be negatively affected. Our personal and work relationships may suffer.

Taoism and Entanglement

In Taoism, it's clearly recognized that entanglement with the various activities of the world leads to significant problems and chronic stress. It puts us out of harmony because our excessive activities cause us to lose our root and center. Just as practicing wuwei is a Taoist solution to the problem of interfering with ourselves and others, practicing *wushi*, or not getting entangled in the activities of the world, is a Taoist solution to the problem of being entangled with, controlled by, and enamored with the activities of the world. In both cases, the first step of the solution is to simply become aware of the fact that we have a problem.

Martha's Story

About six months ago, at the suggestion of a number of friends, Martha bought a smartphone. She discovered how easy and enjoyable it was to text. She loved texting and often got up early and went to bed late so she could text her friends, who were scattered all over the country, and let them know how she was and what she'd been doing. Her life began to revolve around texting. She texted when she ate, and to make more time for texting, she started eating mainly prepared foods, including a lot of fast food. Whenever she got a chance, she even texted while she was at work. She started getting frustrated with anything that took time away from texting.

One morning when Martha's alarm went off, she reached over, dazed and groggy, turned it off, and fell back to sleep. Sometime later her phone rang with a specific tone that let her know someone was texting her. She rolled out of bed, picked up her phone, and read the text. It was from a coworker: *u r late 4 work. where r u?* Martha panicked and looked at the clock. She was already half an hour late for work. She had been late for work three times in the last two weeks. In addition, her boss had expressed concerns that her work performance was going downhill.

Martha's head started to throb. She could feel cold sweat all over her body, her stomach was churning, and she felt drained. She texted back: *I m on way. Traffic.* She then noticed that her wrist was sore, her fingers and thumb felt stiff and painful, and her neck and shoulder hurt. These aches and pains were getting to be a regular occurrence and sometimes persisted for an hour or longer. She threw on some clothes, grabbed an iced coffee drink from her refrigerator, and headed down the stairs of her apartment, texting her friends about her current status as she went. She missed the last step and fell into the wall, bruising her shoulder and knee. She was relieved that her phone wasn't damaged.

Martha got into her car, put her phone on the seat next to her, and began hurriedly driving to work. Her phone rang while she was driving. She looked down at it and saw that it was another text from her coworker. As she reached for her phone to respond, she was hit broadside by a car. She had just driven through a red light.

Practice   Examining Your Entanglement with the Activities of the World

This exercise will help you bring possible entanglement problems to the surface so you can examine them as potential sources of chronic stress. Begin by reflecting upon your activities in the world. What are you involved with? Working? Volunteering? Surfing the Web? Gaming? Texting? Make a list of all of the major activities you engage in.

Next, answer the following eleven questions for each activity you listed. These questions will help you identify activities that may be contributing to chronic stress. As mentioned, in the Taoist approach the first step is to become aware of the problem. Simply insert each activity you've listed in the blank area in each question (you can do this mentally). Record your answers in your journal. When you've responded to all eleven questions for one activity, go back and repeat the process for the next activity until you've worked through your entire list. This process might take a while, so feel free to work on it over the course of several sessions.

1. Does participating and engaging in _____ consume an excessive amount of your time, such that other aspects of your life are affected negatively because you don't have enough time to attend to them?

2. As a result of participating and engaging in _____, do you notice any physical pain?

3. As a result of participating and engaging in _____, do you notice any problems with your attention, concentration, memory, or thinking in other areas of your life?

4. As a result of participating and engaging in _____, do you find that you have problems with patience, anger, anxiety, or depression in other areas of your life?

5. As a result of participating and engaging in _____, do you find that you aren't getting enough restful sleep?

6. As a result of participating and engaging in _____, do you find that you are often tired or lack energy in other areas of your life?

7. As a result of participating and engaging in _____, do you find that you skip meals or don't eat in a healthy manner?

8. As a result of participating and engaging in _____, do you find that you don't exercise?

9. As a result of participating and engaging in _____, do you find that your face-to-face interpersonal relationships with friends, family, coworkers, and others suffer?

10. Do you find that participating and engaging in _____ negatively interferes with your job?

11. When you aren't able to participate and engage in _____, do you become stressed?

Answering yes to any of these questions indicates that you are entangled with and negatively influenced by that particular activity. A yes answer sends a message about your chronic stress.

Reducing or Eliminating Entanglement with Activities

The solution to excessive problematic behaviors is wushi: not being entangled in the activities of the world. To practice wushi, you need to reduce or eliminate excessive problematic behaviors and thereby simplify your life. The choice about whether to reduce or completely eliminate an activity depends on your situation, the specific activity, and the problems it's causing.

Whether you reduce or eliminate the activity, you'll get time back—time that you need to devote to other areas of your life. It's important that you use this recovered time in a way that's beneficial for your overall well-being and health by restoring balance in your life. Of course, you must also be vigilant that you don't become entangled in these other activities; otherwise you'll get stuck in the same insidious trap.

Whether your goal is to eliminate the behavior or just reduce the amount of time you spend engaging in it, the process is essentially the same. The major difference is that if you choose to just reduce the behavior, you need to monitor whether its damaging effects do indeed decrease. For example, say you're trying to heal a repetitive strain injury due to excessive gaming. If you choose the approach of reducing and not eliminating the behavior of gaming, you need to closely monitor whether the injury and pain are improving. Depending on the overall negative impact of the activity and the intensity of your stress, simply reducing the amount of time you engage in the problematic activity may or may not be adequate. You be the judge.

When you first notice the desire to engage in the entangling activity or notice thoughts about it arising, simply inhale and let out a big sigh. Then take three deep breaths and let out a big sigh each time you exhale. If thoughts start coming into your mind while you're focused on breathing, remember to practice guan and smile. Don't engage the thoughts; simply acknowledge that they occurred without making any judgments about them, and then return to your breathing. If you're focused on smiling and breathing deeply, the desire to engage in the activity will subside as you cease thinking about it.

The environment or context you are in may play a significant role in your entanglement with the activities of the world. To investigate this, maintain guan and smile as you scan your environment. See if you can locate anything in your environment that may be pulling you to engage in the entangling activity. Can you change your environment so the pull isn't so intense, or perhaps even eliminate whatever is creating that pull? If you can, make the change.

If this isn't possible and you can't avoid the environment, make sure you practice guan and smile whenever you enter that environment. This will help you change how you relate to that environment and the pull it exerts on you to engage in the problematic activity. Remember to focus on your breath, especially on sighing as you exhale, when you find yourself in challenging environments and notice the desire to engage in the activity beginning to arise.

By continuing to practice deep breathing, sighing as you exhale, guan, and smiling, you'll gradually start to reduce or eliminate the feelings, thoughts, or desires that contribute to engaging in the entangling and stressful behavior. Be aware that it will take some time. Don't rush it. Be patient.

Tom's Story

It was 9 p.m. when Tom dragged himself into the house. His wife, Hannah, glared at him and said, "Where have you been? Don't you know what night this is?" Tom, somewhat startled, said, "I told you I was going to be working with the group this week on our environmental awareness exhibit for next month. So what's the problem?"

Infuriated, Hannah replied, " You've been spending all of your free time this week, as you did last week, with that damn group. The week before that, it was your world peace society. Before that, it was your end hunger organization. It never stops! We've been talking about this for months. I'm tired of you ignoring our family. You said you understood, and last Friday you promised me and the kids that we'd all go out to dinner and a movie tonight. We waited for you, and not only did you not show up, you didn't even call."

Tom said, "I got caught up in our meeting. It was a long agenda. Besides, protecting the environment is really important— and more important for our kids' future. How can you not see that?"

Hannah was dumbfounded and said, "But right now, it's also important to your kids to know that you care enough about them to make time for them." Tom looked away and said he had a headache and was tired. He went into the bathroom to get some aspirin, and Hannah followed him. She told him, "Tomorrow night, we're all going to go out, as a family, to have dinner and see a movie."

Tom replied, "I can't. We have a really important meeting tomorrow. How about if we go out with some of our friends and their families this weekend? You used to really like that. I'm sure you can arrange something."

Hannah couldn't believe what she was hearing. She responded, "*Our* friends? You mean *my* friends. We haven't been out with my friends and their families for months because they don't want to spend time with you. All you do is talk about all of your various causes and all the time you spend on them. If that isn't bad enough, you then try to get them to give money to these causes. They don't want to listen to you. They want to have some fun when they go out. They don't want to go out with you."

Tom replied, "I don't understand. These are such important causes. Why can't they see this? They must be self-centered. They obviously don't care about anyone else."

Hannah said, "We're going out tomorrow. Be home at five so you can get ready. Tell your group you won't be there." Then she turned and went to bed.

Tom was seething. His head was sore, his heart was pounding, and his stomach was queasy. He hadn't eaten much over the past few days. He took his aspirin with a beer. Then he got on the computer and spent the next five hours reading and posting comments on various online message boards about various issues he was working on. Finally, at 2:30 a.m., he went to bed.

The next day, Tom's boss saw him using the company computer to email members of an environmental group. She walked up to Tom and said, "This is your last warning. Don't use company time and the company computer for your personal interests. I've just watched you waste twenty minutes of company time. The next time I catch you, you will be fired. Do you understand?" Tom nodded quietly, but inside he was so angry he felt like he might explode.

After work, Tom dragged himself to the meeting of the environmental group and vented his frustration with his self-centered and uncaring boss. When he finally got home at a little after 10 p.m., no one was there. A note on the table simply said, "Wrong choice!"

Interlude

Now that we've explored wushi, not getting entangled in the activities of the world, from a mental perspective, it's time to turn to the physical approach. In this approach, the focus isn't consciously directed toward disentanglement from problematic activities. The focus is on stretching, loosening, and relaxing the body. From the Taoist perspective, this approach not only centers, roots, and calms the body; it also stills the mind and empties it of agitation. As a result, the process of getting entangled in the activities of the world is gradually removed and the chronic stress associated with it is eliminated.

Qigong

If you are in some way entangled in the activities of the world, the practice of qigong will assist you in disentangling yourself. Aside from all the benefits of qigong previously mentioned, the simple fact that you are practicing qigong on a regular and consistent basis redistributes your time, hopefully allocating time previously spent in the problematic, entangling behavior toward the purpose of putting your life back in balance. Of course, you certainly don't want to get entangled with the practice of qigong.

In this section, in addition to learning the next posture in the Baduanjin and Yijinjing sequences, you'll first learn a posture from the Sun style of taijiquan, which is also the foundational posture of the Sun style of taijiqigong. The purpose of this posture, aside from calming the mind and body, is to acquaint you with the experience of feeling qi.

After first practicing each of the three new postures and linking the sixth postures of Baduanjin and Yijinjing to the sequences, reflect upon your experiences while performing it. What were your body and mind telling you about yourself? Take some time to write in your journal about what you experienced while performing these movements.

Practice Posture 1 of the Sun Style Taijiqigong Sequence: Pulling Qi Left and Right

While performing this posture (adapted from Santee 2010), practice guan and smile throughout. Begin in the Wuji Standing position (the first posture of the Yijinjing sequence), with your hands hanging down at your sides and your palms facing the outside of your thighs. Breathing naturally, shift your weight to your right foot and step out to the side with your left foot so that your feet are shoulder-width apart. Your knees should be aligned with your toes, and your weight should be evenly distributed. Inhaling, move your arms forward, letting them slowly rise up until they reach the height of your shoulders, fingertips pointing forward and palms facing each other about a head-width apart. It should look as if your hands are holding a large ball. Gaze between your hands.

From this position, exhale and bend your elbows, bringing your hands back toward your chest until they are approximately an extended thumb's distance from your chest, with your fingers pointing straight up and your hands perpendicular to your forearms. Twist the little finger of each hand slightly inward. The distance between your palms should still be about a head-width.

Inhale and slowly separate your hands until your thumbs are in line with your shoulders. This contracts the back by bringing the shoulder blades together, which expands and opens the chest. Visualize your entire body, from your feet to the top of your head, expanding, like a balloon being blown up, as you inhale. Pause slightly when your thumbs come into alignment with your shoulders. Keep your elbows down and your shoulders relaxed.

After pausing, exhale and slowly push your hands inward, returning to the position in front of your chest about a head-width apart. This contracts or closes your chest and expands or opens your back as your shoulder blades return to their original position. As you exhale, visualize your entire body, from your feet to the top of your head, contracting, like a balloon from which the air is slowly being let out.

Moving your hands from head-width to shoulder-width apart and back constitutes one repetition. Repeat six more times, for a total of seven repetitions. After the last repetition, lower your hands and return to the Wuji Standing position.

Upon returning to Wuji Standing, reflect on your experience. When you expanded and contracted your hands, did you feel as if the fingers and palms of your hands were connected by elastic or taffy as they moved away from and toward each other? Did you sense any warmth, tingling, or pulsating in your fingers or palms?

As your hands moved together, did you have a sensation of resistance between your fingers and palms, as if you were pushing against something from both sides? Did it feel as though you were pushing against a balloon or ball? Even though you didn't see anything between your fingers and palms, did you feel as though something was there?

All of these sensations and feelings are acquainting you with the flow of qi. Because the focal point of this posture is in line with the center of your chest, and because the center of your chest, or middle dantian, is an area where qi is stored, this posture gathers, cultivates, and circulates qi.

If you don't initially feel any of these sensations, that's perfectly okay. Don't try to force anything, and don't think about anything. Just feel, continue to smile and apply guan, and practice consistently and regularly. It may take some time.

This posture is a clear representation of the process of yin and yang as you expand (yang) your hands to the sides and contract (yin) them to the center. The practice coordinates your breathing with your hand movements and integrates mind and body while training attention and concentration. Your mind will still and empty out. This posture allows you to center and root. It is a very simple and straight-forward way to reduce chronic stress and relax mind and body.

Practice Posture 6 of the Baduanjin Sequence: Massaging Your Lower Back

From the posture Sitting in Stillness, which you returned to after the posture Swishing Saliva in Your Mouth Thirty-Six Times, bring your hands together in front of you, allowing your palms and fingers to touch each other. Rub them back and forth until they feel hot. Place them on your skin at the small of your back and rub them up and down your lower back a total of thirty-six times. Return your hands to their original position on your lap or thighs. Focus on the warmth in your lower back area and see if you can visualize the fire from your heart sinking down to your lower dantian, located three inches below your belly button.

The function of this posture is to help relieve pain in the lower back. Consistent practice of this posture will strengthen your kidneys and your waist.

Practice Posture 6 of the Yijinjing Sequence: Pushing Out Your Claws and Showing Your Wings

While performing this posture, inhale through your nose, exhale through your mouth, and keep your focus on your hands. From the Wuji Standing posture, which you returned to after the posture Supporting a Staff Above Your Head, slowly take a deep breath, clench your fists with palms facing up, and slowly draw them up your sides, with your elbows pointing behind you, until your fists reach your armpits. Your back will be contracted, and your chest will be expanded.

Keeping your hands and fingers tight, open up your fists, palms still facing up, so that your fingers point forward. Begin to slowly exhale. At the same time, slowly expand your back and contract your chest to push your hands forward. As you push, rotate your hands inward and upward until your fingers are pointing up and your palms are facing forward. The tips of your fingers should be even with your shoulders. Continue to push forward as if you're pushing against a wall. Your entire upper body, including your fingers, hands, arms, and shoulders, is held in dynamic tension. At full extension your elbows should remain slightly bent; don't lock your elbows.

While slowly taking a deep breath, clench your fists and rotate your hands outward until your palms are facing up. Maintaining the dynamic tension, exhale and slowly pull your fists back to your armpits.

This sequence, from fists at your armpits to palms facing forward and back again, constitutes one repetition. Maintaining the dynamic tension, repeat this sequence six more times, for a total of seven repetitions. When you've finished the last repetition, take a deep breath, then slowly exhale while lowering your fists down your sides. Gradually open them and release the tension as you return to the Wuji Standing posture.

This posture provides the type of dynamic tension associated with anaerobic exercise. Aside from developing your attention and concentration and strengthening your upper body, shoulders, arms, and fingers, this posture enhances the breath, the circulation of blood, and the circulation of qi.

Conclusion

This chapter explored the Taoist practice of wushi, or not getting entangled in the activities of the world, and examined how ongoing excessive entanglement with the activities of the world puts us out of harmony and results in chronic stress. This process is so insidious that it can be difficult to see the link between entanglement in activities of the world and chronic stress. The next chapter will look at how changing thoughts and behaviors and reducing desires can be integrated into a single process for reducing chronic stress. As you read on, remember to smile and practice guan.

Chapter 8

Changing Your Thoughts and Behaviors and Reducing Your Desires

This chapter explores the mental approach to changing thoughts and behaviors and reducing desires. It will take a somewhat different approach from most of the previous chapters. The entire discussion of the mental approach is presented in the context of stories. This type of presentation—discussing ideas, concepts, techniques, and practices via stories—is an ancient Taoist approach to teaching and learning. Through the stories in this chapter, you'll see how changing thoughts, changing behaviors, and reducing desires are interdependent and developed in an integrated way. The stories in this chapter present these processes within the context of practicing wuwei (not interfering with yourself or others), guan (nonjudgmental awareness and insight), wushi (not getting entangled in the affairs of the world), and balancing excessive yang behavior with yin behavior.

Through these stories, you'll come to see the link between the first two components of the Taoist path: simplifying life and reducing desires. Ultimately, though, the focus is on changing or eliminating behavior that results in chronic stress. Be it thoughts, judgments, beliefs, negativity, feelings, desires, or actions, it is still behavior that needs to be eliminated or changed.

Rebecca's Story

Rebecca's coworkers weren't behaving as she thought they should. She had repeatedly asked them to turn in their reports a couple of days early so she could review them, but they wouldn't comply. She couldn't understand why they wouldn't do whatever was needed to meet her request, such as getting to work early or leaving late. It would be more efficient, and it would also make her life easier and less stressful. Rebecca had attended a class on how to optimally manage a business and had also done a lot of reading on the topic, so she was sure she was correct and her coworkers and boss were wrong. She had complained to her boss about the situation, but he was no help and actually agreed with her coworkers.

Rebecca was extremely frustrated and thought about quitting, but given the current high unemployment rates, she was worried she might not easily find a new job. When she complained to her friends about her work problems, they weren't sympathetic. In fact, they told her to stop whining and suggested that she might be the one with a problem. She was outraged that her supposed friends didn't support her and wondered why they didn't behave the way they were supposed to. Eventually, Rebecca felt overwhelmed by how often others didn't meet her expectations. She started having problems with attention, concentration, sleep, and appetite. She felt tense and drained most of the time. She was clearly stressed.

Rebecca knew she had a problem, so she searched online for different approaches to dealing with stress. One item was an article on qigong, which discussed deep breathing, managing stress, learning how to relax, and performing certain repetitious movements in a slow, rhythmic way. She thought, *That sounds quite easy. It's all about stretching. It's nothing profound. There's really not much to it.* She read a few more articles on qigong, and after finishing them, she thought she understood it pretty well and felt it wouldn't take long to learn how to do it. The articles recommended a few books on qigong, and she decided to go to a bookstore to buy them so she'd have a really strong foundation in qigong. As she approached the cash register, she was aghast. The line was so long. Didn't anybody care? It reminded her of when she went to the grocery store and always ended up in a long line. The inefficiency drove her nuts and made her really angry.

When Rebecca finished reading the books, she felt she knew a lot about qigong. Remembering that she had seen a sign about qigong classes two doors down from her workplace, she decided to look into the classes after work the next day. She wondered if they really knew about qigong.

When Rebecca walked into the office, she saw a lady sitting with her back to her. Rebecca said, "Is someone in charge here?" The lady slowly turned around. With a big smile on her face, she softly motioned to Rebecca to sit down across from her. Rebecca, who was clearly impatient, addressed the woman rather brusquely. "I don't really have a lot of time. Because I've read a lot about qigong, I just want to know what type of qigong you teach, how you teach it, when you have classes, and how much they cost."

The lady looked at her and gently said, "Why did you bring so many people with you?"

Somewhat startled, Rebecca turned around. Seeing nothing, looked back at the lady and anxiously said, "I didn't bring anybody. There's nobody behind me. What do you mean?"

The lady, still smiling, warmly responded, "And so many opinions, beliefs, and judgments. My, oh my. Such stress!" Rebecca felt quite nervous, and her mouth got very dry. The lady then said, "I need to ask you a couple of questions. Then I will answer your questions. Is that okay?" Rebecca nodded.

The lady took out a small teacup, filled it to the brim with water, and handed it to Rebecca. Then she said, "If I wanted to offer you some tea to drink from this cup, what would you need to do?" Rebecca indicated that she'd need to empty out the teacup. The lady asked, "Why?"

Somewhat arrogantly, Rebecca replied, "Because the cup is filled with water. There's no room to pour any tea into it. Obviously it needs to be empty."

The lady calmly said, "Let's try a qigong exercise. Is that okay with you?"

Rebecca muttered, "It's about time," under her breath, then bluntly responded, "Fine!"

The lady gently said, "I want you to close your eyes and just sit for two minutes and not think. Okay?"

Rebecca said, "No problem," and shut her eyes. Within seconds, thoughts were racing through her mind: *This is stupid, What a waste of time, I didn't see this in the books or articles I read, Talking about people behind me and empty tea cups—I don't get it*, and on and on. The more she ruminated, the more stressed she got.

The lady calmly said, "Time is up." When Rebecca opened her eyes, the lady asked her how she did and how she felt. Rebecca replied, "Not very well, I guess. My mind was full of thoughts."

With great tenderness, the lady said, "Now I'd like you to sit up straight, close your eyes, and breathe slowly. Every time you exhale, count quietly to yourself. Start with one and work up to fifteen. If you get distracted by a thought, don't make any judgments about it; just return to your breathing. If you lose count, just start over at one. The important thing is not to dwell on anything. Just stay focused on your breath and counting. Are you okay with this?"

Rebecca nodded, and the lady told her to begin. After two minutes, the lady told her to stop. Rebecca opened her eyes, smiled, and said, " I feel different—more relaxed. I got distracted, but I returned to my breath and counting, and I didn't get stuck in my thoughts."

The lady, smiling broadly, looked directly into Rebecca's eyes and said, "You came into this office filled to the brim with opinions, beliefs, and judgments about not only qigong but, I suspect, almost everything. When your mind is filled to the brim, it is closed and restricted, which isn't conducive to learning qigong. It needs to be emptied out so you can learn. Because your mind is so agitated, which makes you quite aggressive, you are excessively yang in nature and thus not in harmony. I needed you to experience this, so I gave you the breathing exercise to move you out of your agitated thoughts and into a direct experience of your body. The breathing exercise is yin in nature and allows you to experience the connection between your feelings and not dwelling on thoughts. As a result, your yin and yang started to harmonize and you felt more relaxed. This is just the starting point. Achieving greater balance and harmony will take time."

Rebecca, still smiling peacefully, said, "I don't know what to say other than thank you—and how can I sign up for classes?"

David's Story

David liked to bowl. In fact, he was quite good. Unfortunately, whenever he went bowling with friends, he did quite poorly. He became excessively self-conscious and stressed himself out. He felt tense, sweated profusely, and got an upset stomach, and his mouth would get so dry that he could hardly talk to others. Within himself, he felt excessive self-doubt and told himself that he really wasn't very good, that he was lucky if he managed to knock a few pins down, and that he wasn't on par with his friends. Truth be told, David felt this way almost any time he was around other people.

One day while he was bowling by himself, his friend Daoling happened to be in the bowling alley. David didn't see him, and Daoling stood some distance off, watching David bowl. He noticed that David was very good and quite relaxed—nothing like when he bowled with friends. Daoling watched David make strike after strike.

When David finished his game, Daoling walked up and told him he was a fantastic bowler. David was startled and felt both pleased and somewhat embarrassed. David couldn't recall when anyone had last given him such a nice compliment.

Daoling asked David how he could be so good when he bowled by himself and so different when he bowled with others. David felt self-conscious, but he decided to tell Daoling about how he usually worried about his behavior whenever he was around others. Daoling asked David what he thought about when he was bowling alone. David said he didn't think about anything. His mind was blank. He just focused on his stance, his approach, and releasing the ball. He didn't think about it; he just did it. Next, Daoling asked David what he thought about when he was bowling and friends were around. David said, "They're looking at me and judging me, and I'm not a good bowler." Daoling asked David if he saw any connection with what was going on in his mind and how well he bowled in the two situations. After thinking it over for a moment, David realized that he was getting in his own way—that his mind was interfering—when he bowled with others.

Daoling smiled and then told David that he'd had similar experiences with being excessively self-conscious and stressed-out as a result. He said, "My father wanted to help, so he took me to a taijiquan class. At first it didn't seem to help. As far as I was concerned, in the taijiquan class people were still watching me. Nothing really changed until the instructor came up to me and told me about the practice of wuwei, which means not interfering with yourself. The instructor helped me start applying wuwei by directing me to focus on my hands and breath while I moved through the various forms. He said that if my mind wandered or started to engage in self-doubt or self-criticism, instead of making judgments about it, I should just refocus on my hands and breath. It took a while, but after consistent and regular practice, I was able to stop interfering with myself while practicing taijiquan. Then, gradually, I applied that same approach to other parts of my life, focusing on my breathing and being nonjudgmental. Since then, I've been able to mostly free myself from self-consciousness and self-doubt. Does that make sense?"

David smiled and nodded. Daoling smiled back. Then he took David by the arm and said, "So, how about if we bowl together? I can watch and help you help yourself." David agreed, and thus his journey into the practice of wuwei began.

Tiande's Story

Tiande had been feeling tired for some time. He wasn't eating much, and his sleep was poor. He couldn't understand what was going on. At his annual checkup a couple of months ago, his doctor said there was no apparent medical cause for Tiande's symptoms, but that he did appear to be somewhat stressed. He suggested that Tiande take a look at stressors in his life. He told him about a stress management program the hospital offered and recommended that Tiande look into it. He thanked his doctor for the advice, but he had no intention of attending a stress management program. He had a good job and made a lot of money. He wasn't bouncing all over the place and screaming. How could he be stressed?

As Tiande sat in his office at home wondering about his lack of energy, he started thinking about his upbringing. His mother was quite yang, or Confucian, always seeming to be in charge and keeping everything organized. She believed there was a proper way to behave in every situation. She was very focused on family and social harmony, on her kids getting a good education, and on working hard. His father, on the other hand, was very yin, or Taoist, in nature and advocated moderation, staying healthy, taking care of oneself, not getting entangled in society, being in harmony with nature, and not interfering with oneself. Tiande realized his parents had provided him with a good balance between the Confucian yang and the Taoist yin throughout his childhood. It dawned on him that now he was out of harmony. He was, in a sense, too Confucian, or yang. He needed balance from Taoism. He needed to be more yin.

Tiande decided to take a look at his life. He got out a piece of paper and started to describe his current life. When he read what he'd written, he was stunned. Essentially, all he did was work excessively long hours. He didn't really do anything else. He didn't have close friends or a family of his own. He was excessively entangled with his work world. He thought back and saw that he'd gradually increased his work hours until he was always the first to arrive and the last to leave.

As he reflected upon this, it hit him that his lack of energy, poor sleep, and loss of appetite were all linked to working excessively. He was clearly out of harmony. He finally understood that stress wasn't just bouncing all over the place and screaming. It could be quite subtle. In his case, it arose from his entanglement in his excessive behavior of working long hours, and it was breaking down his body and mind.

With sadness, Tiande realized that he didn't need the additional money he earned from all of those extra hours, and that no one was forcing him to work so much or even asking him to. He could work a regular schedule if he wanted. Tiande understood that he needed to explore why he worked so much. But for now, he was relieved to see a pathway toward getting his energy and health back: eliminating his excessive involvement with work. Then and there, he made a commitment to finding other activities to engage in so he could restore some balance to his life.

Janet's Story

As Janet raced up to her apartment carrying two shopping bags full of newly purchased clothes, she saw her neighbor, Mr. Wu. She really liked him. As usual, he was smiling and looked very calm. Janet wished she could feel that way. She wished she wasn't so driven to shop and buy new things she didn't really need, especially because she ended up feeling so guilty about her out-of-control shopping that her purchases didn't bring her as much enjoyment as she thought they would.

Mr. Wu looked at Janet kindly and said that she seemed to be somewhat on edge. Since she had known Mr. Wu and his wife for some time, Janet decided to tell him about her problem. As she explained her problem, Mr. Wu listened and nodded a few times but didn't say anything. When she finished speaking, he said, "After you put your things away, why don't you come over to my apartment to have some tea with me and my wife?"

Janet gratefully accepted his invitation. She had been to the Wus' apartment a few times before and had always found it to be quite peaceful. It was decorated very simply, with several scrolls, a couple of ceramic statues, and a gurgling fountain. Everything seemed to be in harmony. Mrs. Wu, whose smile was even brighter than Mr. Wu's, greeted her at the door, then gently touched her elbow and guided her to a round table where Mr. Wu was preparing tea.

As Janet sat down, she noticed that Mr. Wu's movements were slow and peaceful, yet focused. After preparing the tea in a small teapot, he poured it into three tiny cups. Handing Janet her cup, he recommended that she first take a deep breath and slowly let it out, then look at the cup, then close her eyes and smell the tea—all before taking her first sip. As Janet tried this approach, she felt her stress melt away. Mr. Wu asked Janet how she was feeling, and she said she hadn't felt so relaxed in a long time. She said it seemed like time had slowed down.

Then Mr. Wu asked Janet if she felt comfortable enough to tell Mrs. Wu about the problem she'd discussed with him. Janet said she did, and that she hoped Mrs. Wu could help her.

After Janet described her problematic shopping, Mrs. Wu nodded. Then she asked Janet if it was okay if she offered some observations. Janet said, "Please do." Mrs. Wu then said that, in general, aside from Janet's concern about her excessive shopping, Janet appeared to be somewhat hyperactive and fairly stressed. Janet agreed.

Mrs. Wu said, "The fact that you recognize that you have a problem with excessive desires to buy clothes you don't need and want to make a change is the most important step. Equally important, you have acknowledged that you are challenged by prolonged stress and being somewhat hyperactive. The next time you are in a clothing store and start to think about your desire to buy something you don't need or start to feel the anxiety linked to your desires, try this: Slowly let out a big sigh. Observe how you feel. Then do that two more times, taking deep breaths and sighing as you exhale. Take another moment to observe how you feel, and then simply walk away."

Mrs. Wu then said, "One more thing. It's important to smile while you exhale slowly and let out a big sigh. If you are focused on smiling and sighing as you slowly exhale, you'll feel relaxed. Your thoughts about buying the clothes will diminish, and as a result, your desire to buy the clothes will subside. Over time, this will help you get rid of the stress associated with your desires."

Interlude

As you were reading the stories in the first half of this chapter, you consciously focused, from an intentional, cognitive standpoint, or yang perspective, on the relationship between thoughts, beliefs, desires, behaviors, noninterference (wuwei), and not getting entangled in the affairs of the world (wushi) and considered how these interrelated factors are involved in chronic stress. Now it's time to turn your attention to the meditative or qigong viewpoint, which is the yin perspective. Here too the goal is to remove chronic stress from a balanced and harmonious perspective consistent with Taoist teachings.

From the physical standpoint, the focus isn't consciously directed toward the relationship between thoughts, beliefs, desires, behaviors, noninterference, and not getting entangled in the affairs of the world. Rather, the focus is on calming and relaxing the body in order to still the mind and empty it of agitation. The physical practice also establishes harmony and balance by allowing qi to circulate freely, without obstructions.

Qigong

In this section, in addition to learning the seventh posture in both the Baduanjin and Yijinjing sequences, you'll learn the second posture from the Sun style of taijiqigong. This posture continues the exploration of the activation and circulation of qi initiated with the first posture of the Sun style of taijiqigong: Pulling Qi Left and Right. The slight difference between the first posture and the second will help you learn how to activate and circulate qi within a different framework. As you work with different frameworks, or postures, you'll increase the depth of your sensation of qi.

After first practicing each of the three new postures and linking the seventh postures of the Baduanjin and Yijinjing to the sequences, reflect upon your experiences while performing each. What were your body and mind telling you about yourself? Take some time to write in your journal about what you experienced while performing these movements.

Practice   Posture 2 of the Sun Style Taijiqigong Sequence: Moving Qi Up and Down

Remember to practice guan and smile throughout your practice of this posture—and all qigong. From the Wuji Standing position, which you returned to after the first posture, Pulling Qi Left and Right, begin in the same way as you did in the previous posture: Breathing naturally, shift your weight to your right foot and step out to the side with your left foot so that your feet are shoulder-width apart and your weight is evenly distributed. Inhaling, move your arms forward, letting them slowly rise up until they reach the height of your shoulders, fingertips pointing forward and palms facing each other about a head-width apart. Gaze between your hands.

From this position, exhale and bend your elbows, bringing your hands back toward your chest until your hands are approximately an extended thumb's distance from your chest, with your fingers pointing straight up and your hands perpendicular to your forearms. Twist the little finger of each hand slightly inward. The distance between your palms should still be about a head-width. Visualize holding a ball between your hands.

Slowly rotate this imaginary ball until your left hand is on top and your right hand is on the bottom, keeping your palms facing each other and maintaining the distance between them. Your left hand should be line with the middle of your sternum, and your right hand should be in line with your solar plexus. Make sure your shoulders are relaxed and down and your elbows are hanging down, not pointing to the sides.

As you slowly take a deep breath, slowly and gently separate your hands, pulling your left hand up under your jaw and your right hand down just below the level of your belly button. Keep your palms facing each other as your hands separate. Visualize your entire body, from the soles of your feet to the top of your head, slowly expanding, like a balloon being blown up, as you inhale. Pause briefly.

As you slowly and gently exhale, simultaneously slowly and gently lower your left hand and raise your right hand until you return to the original position of holding a ball with your left hand on top and right hand on the bottom, palms still facing each other. Visualize your entire body, from the soles of your feet to the top of your head, slowly contracting, like a balloon from which the air is slowly being let out.

Repeat six more times, for a total of seven repetitions, slowly and gently pulling your hands apart as you inhale, then slowly and gently pushing them back together as you exhale. After the last repetition, simply rotate the ball, keeping the distance between your palms the same, until your left hand is on the bottom and your right hand is on top. Then repeat the same sequence, starting and ending in this new position, for a total of seven repetitions.

After finishing the seventh repetition, pull your elbows inward and rotate your hands so that the fingertips of both hands point up, with your palms still facing each other and the distance between your palms remaining about a head-width apart. Then lower your hands and return to the Wuji Standing position.

As in the previous chapter, reflect on your experience. Did you experience any sensations between your fingers and palms as they slowly separated and moved toward each other? Did they feel connected to each other? Did you sense any warmth, tingling, or pulsating in your fingers?

As your hands moved together, did you have a sensation of resistance between your fingers and palms, as if you were pushing against something from above and below? Did it feel as though you were pushing against a balloon or ball? Even though you didn't see anything between your fingers and palms, did you feel as though something was there?

As noted in the previous chapter, all of these sensations and feelings are acquainting you with the flow of qi. If you don't initially feel any of these sensations, that's perfectly okay. Don't try to force anything and don't think about anything. Just feel, continue to smile and apply guan, and practice consistently and regularly. It may take some time.

Practice   Posture 7 of the Baduanjin Sequence: Rowing a Boat

From the Sitting in Stillness posture, which you returned to after the posture Massaging Your Lower Back, uncurl your legs. Straighten them and extend them in front of you, feet about shoulder-width apart, with your toes pointing up.

Fold your thumbs into your palms and close your fingers around them. Then gently push your hands forward at shoulder height, right arm over your right leg, and left arm over your left leg. Your arms should be parallel to each other and to your legs.

Now imagine that you're in a rowboat and each hand is grasping an oar. Keeping your legs straight out in front of you, inhale deeply and slowly and gently rotate both of your shoulders forward and then upward. Then, exhaling slowly, rotate your shoulders back and then down. Repeat six more times.

After finishing the seventh repetition, roll your shoulders in the opposite direction. As you inhale deeply, slowly and gently rotate your shoulders back and then upward. Then exhale slowly and rotate your shoulders forward and then down. Repeat six more times. After you finish the seventh repetition, let your arms come to rest in your lap.

This posture loosens and opens your shoulders and stretches your sides. Make sure you practice guan and smile throughout all of the repetitions.

Practice Posture 7 of the Yijinjing Sequence: Nine Ghosts Pulling a Saber

From the Wuji Standing posture, which you returned to after the posture Pushing Out Your Claws and Showing Your Wings, slowly take a deep breath and step to the left so your feet are shoulder-width apart and parallel. As you inhale, place your left hand on the small of your back with your palm facing out to the rear, and place your right palm on the back of your head with your thumb on your neck and the tips of your index and second finger gently touching your left ear. Keeping both hands in contact with your body, turn your head to the left and look over your left shoulder while pulling your right elbow up and to the back. Then slightly bend to the left. You should feel your right side being stretched from under your armpit down to your waist. Exhale. Breathing naturally, maintain this position for thirty to sixty seconds. (Depending on how you feel, you can shorten or extend the duration.)

Return to the posture Wuji Standing, allowing your hands to gently drop down to your sides. Then repeat on the opposite side: As you inhale, place your right hand on the small of your back, palm facing out to the rear, and your left hand against the back of your head, index and second finger touching your right ear. Look over your right shoulder while pulling your left elbow up and to the back, then slightly bend to the right and feel the stretch in your left side. Exhale. Breathing naturally, maintain this position for thirty to sixty seconds.

After completing both sides, return to the Wuji Standing posture. The function of this posture is to stretch and loosen both sides of the torso and the spine. Make sure you practice guan and smile throughout this posture.

A note on the symbolism of this posture: Ancient Chinese warriors often carried their swords in a sheath or scabbard strapped on their back. In order to draw it, they had to reach over their head with one hand to grasp the handle of the sword and reach behind the lower back with the other hand to hold the scabbard in place. The Chinese character and tone for the number nine (jiu) provides a symbolic description of the stretching and energy directions of this movement. In Chinese culture, ghosts are believed to live between heaven and earth. The ghost reference in this posture is to the space between the upper hand (heaven) and the lower hand (earth).

Conclusion

I hope the alternative format of the information in this chapter was a pleasant change of pace, and that it was beneficial to your understanding of the Taoist teachings and your application of those teachings in your own life for your own health and well-being. In the next chapter we will explore the third component of the Taoist path to eliminating chronic stress: emptying and stilling the mind.

Part 4

Stilling and Emptying Your Mind

Chapter 9

The Taoist Body-Based Meditative Core

This chapter explores the nonspecific, nonintentional, and body-grounded Taoist approach to managing and eliminating chronic stress: the meditative core. In the previous six chapters, you consciously focused on specific areas that Taoists, over the ages, have isolated as causing and maintaining chronic stress. From a mental perspective, you examined and analyzed how specific factors, such as absolute thoughts and beliefs and excessive or deficient desires and behaviors, contribute to chronic stress.

In Taoism, this intentional, cognitive, rational, and analytical mind-based approach, which is essentially yang in nature, is a necessary first step. You need to be aware that you have a problem with chronic stress in the first place. Having brought the problems of chronic stress to the forefront of your attention, you then took the next step: examining the specific problems that lead to chronic stress and determining what causes them. You then created specific solutions to face and manage these problems, to help you eliminate chronic stress and the behaviors associated with it.

Running parallel to this approach, in each chapter you learned qigong practices, which are essentially yin in nature, to help you still and empty your mind, creating another avenue to eliminating chronic stress. I asked you to engage in these practices regularly and in a specific sequence, but I didn't provide a great deal of explanation of these practices. The reason for this is that it's important for you to first discover and experience the benefits of these practices on your own and in your body. The only way to truly understand the body-based approach of the Taoist path is by putting it into practice. Underlying these body-based techniques is the Taoist meditative core—the topic of this chapter.

The Basic Practices of the Meditative Core

While aspects of the basic practices of the Taoist meditative core were initially presented in ancient Taoist texts such as the *Neiye*, suggested in the *Neijing*, alluded to in the *Daodejing*, and expanded upon in the *He Shanggong*, a commentary on the *Daodejing*, it is really in the *Zhuangzi* that the specific, somewhat distinct types of meditation are first presented. In the *Zhuangzi*, which was written over 2,200 years ago, the four basic types of practice in the meditative core are Breathing from Your Heels, Mind Like a Mirror, Heart and Mind Fasting, and Sitting in Oblivion or Forgetfulness. The practice of Sitting in Oblivion or Forgetfulness in the *Zhuangzi* was expanded upon in the eighth-century text the *Zuowanglun* (*Discussions on Sitting in Oblivion or Forgetfulness*).

A key point to keep in mind is that when you practice the body-based approaches of the meditative core repeatedly and consistently, threat-based thinking, absolute thoughts, negative thinking, and excessive or deficient desires and behaviors will naturally disappear, since you aren't specifically focused on them. As a result, chronic stress, which is generated and maintained by these factors, will be eliminated.

For Taoists, both the mind-based approach (yang), which is cognitive, intentional, and consciously focused on the factors that cause and maintain chronic stress, and the body-based approach (yin), which is experiential, nonintentional, and not consciously focused on the factors that cause and maintain chronic stress, are necessary. Yang and yin must be in harmony if you are to experience good health and well-being and, ultimately, cultivate yourself spiritually. To round out and bring balance to your practices for easing chronic stress, in this chapter you'll learn the four practices that compose the Taoist meditative core.

Breathing from Your Heels

Although we've discussed deep breathing in previous chapters, the context in which Breathing from Your Heels is presented in the *Zhuangzi* is somewhat different and more holistic in nature (Guo 1974). It isn't simply an isolated practice or technique. Rather, it is viewed, like all aspects of Taoism, as part of an integrated and interrelated approach to health, well-being, and spirituality. Breathing from Your Heels is seen as being intertwined with restful sleep, eating in a noninterfering manner, and interacting with others and the world in a way that doesn't create chronic stress.

Developing an ongoing, consistent practice of Breathing from Your Heels will result in a deep, penetrating relaxation that empties and stills the mind and releases agitation from both body and mind. As a result, when you lie down to go to sleep, your mind will be free from any expectations, worries, desires, negative thoughts, and threat-based thinking that might interfere with your sleep. Being free from this chronic stress, you will experience deep, uninterrupted, restful sleep. Insofar as your body and mind are free from agitation, you won't interfere with yourself when you eat; you will simply eat in the here and now. In your interactions with others and the world, you will approach and then engage others and situations without self-imposed restrictions or agitation. You will be fully in the present moment and free of chronic stress.

Breathing from Your Heels is contrasted with breathing from the throat, which is a shallow, rigid, heaving type of breathing. People who breathe from the throat aren't anchored, centered, or rooted. Unfortunately, this tends to be the manner in which most people breathe, and it is typically associated with chronic stress.

People who engage in Breathing from Your Heels are anchored, centered, and rooted. This way of breathing is slow, deep, smooth, continuous, even, quiet, and soft and based in the diaphragm. Upon inhalation, the diaphragm pulls down, and as a result, the abdomen pushes out. Upon exhalation, the diaphragm is released and rises up, and as a result, the abdomen retracts. Although I described these basic components of diaphragmatic breathing in chapter 2, Breathing from Your Heels goes further by introducing visualization into the process.

Practice   Breathing from Your Heels

Breathing from Your Heels can be practiced sitting (on the ground or in a chair), standing, or lying. If you're sitting or standing, maintain the proper posture you've learned in this book, with your head being gently pulled up, your shoulders relaxed and down, and your back straight but not rigid, as in the Sitting in Stillness and Wuji Standing postures. If you're lying down, lie on your back with your body similarly aligned. Be sure to smile and apply guan throughout this practice.

Using deep or diaphragmatic breathing, slowly and gently inhale through your nose. As you do so, visualize your breath being slowly and gently pulled down the center of your body through your diaphragm, and then being slowly and gently pushed down through your abdomen, your pelvis, and both legs until it reaches the bottom of your feet, particularly your heels. Pause for a moment, then begin to exhale through your nose by relaxing your diaphragm and visualizing your breath slowly and gently rising up from your heels through your legs, into your pelvis and abdomen, and up through your diaphragm, and then continuing to rise through the center of your body and exiting through your nose. Repeat nine more times, for a total of ten repetitions.

For maximum benefit, practice Breathing from Your Heels consistently and regularly. While doing so, extend your awareness to what you experience while engaged in this practice. Note how you feel during and after the ten repetitions. You may wish to write about this in your journal.

Mind Like a Mirror

Find a mirror, stand in front of it, and look into it. What you see, aside from the part of the room that's in front of the mirror, is your reflection. Now step away from the mirror, look at it from the side, and note what you see and don't see.

You'll see a different part of the room, and you won't see yourself. The mirror doesn't hold on to your reflection. It doesn't store it or constantly replay it. Once you are no longer in front of the mirror, you won't be reflected.

Essentially the mirror is still and empty until something or someone is presented before it. It then becomes filled. When the object or person is removed, the mirror returns to its natural stillness and emptiness. The mirror doesn't hold on to anything. It doesn't get entangled with what it reflects. It simply engages and reflects. Because the mirror is naturally still and empty, it doesn't interfere with itself or the objects or people presented before it. It doesn't judge what it reflects. It simply engages and reflects.

In Taoism, we aim to be like the mirror. When the world presents itself, we engage. We respond to it but don't get entangled with it. We know what we cannot resolve, we accept this, and we are at peace with it. We accept what we cannot avoid, without whining about it, and we deal with it. We don't dwell on or hold on to any of it. When we don't dwell on or hold on to such things, we cannot interfere with ourselves or others. We simply use the mind like a mirror and are empty (Guo 1974).

Using your mind like a mirror is, in essence, the basis for practicing both wuwei (not interfering with yourself or others) and wushi (not getting entangled in the activities of the world). To the extent that you have stilled chronic threat-based thinking, negative thinking, problematic absolute thoughts and beliefs, and excessive or deficient desires and behaviors, your mind will be empty like a mirror. When something presents itself to you, you will engage, reflect, and address whatever appears, without any self-generated interference. Then you'll continue your journey without dwelling on or holding on to anything. In this way, chronic stress dissolves.

Practice   Mind Like a Mirror

The next time you interact with someone, try to visualize your mind as a mirror. Apply guan, smile, and simply try to reflect whatever is presented to you. Present to others whatever you wish to present to them, but do so in a manner that isn't harmful to them. In other words, use positive, neutral, or constructive statements. If you wish to engage in constructive criticism, that's perfectly fine. However, if the other person doesn't listen to you or starts to disagree and gets negative toward you, don't push it. Stop and move on to something else, or simply say good-bye and leave.

If the other person ignores what you're saying or displays negativity toward you, verbal or nonverbal, the situation will be challenging because your immediate perception will be that the other person's behavior presents a threat. This threat will probably set off the fight-or-flight response, and you may find yourself swimming in a sea of unwanted stress. This is why it's important to not dwell on or hold on to the person's negativity, not push the issue, and not get into a heated argument. Rather, simply stop the encounter by moving on to something else or saying good-bye and leaving. The point is to recognize when you're starting to feel stressed and then stop the situation from escalating.

In any case, don't engage in negativity, sarcasm, and so on toward yourself or the other person. Simply use your mind like a mirror and respond to whatever occurs without holding on to it. Be empty.

Note how you feel when you successfully practice Mind Like a Mirror. What do you discover about yourself and your stress? Notice how long you're able to practice, and also note the difference in your experience when you aren't able to approach situations from this stance. You may wish to write about this in your journal. Remember, this practice is new, so it may be a challenge. It takes time to develop Mind Like a Mirror. This is normal.

Heart and Mind Fasting

In a sense similar to the cleansing effect of abstaining from food and drink in order to detoxify the body, the practice of Heart and Mind Fasting is focused on removing selfishness and excessive desires associated with the senses and thoughts, which all give rise to and maintain chronic stress. Thus, Heart and Mind Fasting is about cleansing both body and mind of toxicity and chronic stress.

While it is perfectly normal to desire a comfortable life, replete with wealth, status, tasty food and drink, beautiful things, fine clothes, pleasant sounds, enjoyable interpersonal relationships, health, and long life, these desires may give rise to and maintain chronic stress (Guo 1974). If you find yourself continually stressed-out because you haven't obtained these things, it will be detrimental to your physical, psychological, and interpersonal health and well-being. If you find yourself continually stressed-out because even though you have obtained them you're afraid you're going to lose them, it will be detrimental to your physical, psychological, and interpersonal health and well-being. If you find yourself continually stressed-out because you aren't satisfied with what you have and constantly desire more (in other words, your desires are excessive or you simply don't know when enough is enough), it will be detrimental to your physical, psychological, and interpersonal health and well-being. If you find yourself continually stressed-out because you're entitled, self-centered, or selfish, it will be detrimental to your physical, psychological, and interpersonal health and well-being.

The practice of Heart and Mind Fasting focuses on the link between your senses and your thoughts in regard to problematic or otherwise excessive desires that create stress and then helps remove these desires. In the Taoist view, sensory experiences and thoughts in relationship to desires can cause people to be fragmented and lose their center and root. When this happens, people are scattered, dispersed, and easily distracted. They aren't grounded or focused. Mind, body, and environment aren't in harmony, and the result is chronic stress.

The first step in Heart and Mind Fasting is to unify your attention, concentration, and intention (Guo 1974). Focus simply and only on the practice of Heart and Mind Fasting. Don't get distracted, pulled, or controlled by your senses, their objects, and the desires generated by them. Don't listen to your senses or follow where they attempt to lead you. They will cause you to get stuck, dwelling upon and desiring their objects. They will bring you to a standstill. They only provide you with a limited and fragmented viewpoint. If you find yourself being pulled by your senses and their objects, don't make any judgments about them and don't dwell on them. Don't let them entrap you.

Also, don't get distracted, pulled, or controlled by your thoughts, their objects, and the desires generated by them. Don't listen to your thoughts or follow where they and their objects attempt to lead you. They will cause you to get stuck, dwelling upon and desiring their objects. They will bring you to a standstill. They only provide you with a limited and fragmented viewpoint. If you find yourself being pulled by your thoughts and their objects, don't make any judgments about them and don't dwell on them. Don't let them entrap you.

When you're practicing Heart and Mind Fasting, listen with and attend to your qi, or breath. Unlike your senses and thoughts, qi doesn't have an object for you to desire or to distract you. It won't cause you to get stuck and stop. Qi continually changes as you inhale and exhale, moving through cycles, in and out, in much the same way that existence itself cycles through a process of continual change.

Because qi, or breath, is essentially emptiness, it simply waits for things to occur. Because it has no object, it isn't controlled by objects. Our senses and thoughts, however, do not wait. They attempt to control us and pull us toward their objects. They are continually occupied and thus not empty. They have the potential to create chronic stress.

Tao, the source of everything, has no object. It is empty. Therefore, the practice of Heart and Mind Fasting is to cultivate emptiness within ourselves through our qi, or breath. In so doing, we experientially realize that the emptiness within ourselves is the same as the emptiness of Tao. This is the heart of Taoist spirituality.

Practice   Heart and Mind Fasting

While Heart and Mind Fasting can be practiced anywhere and in any position, I'll introduce you to it using a position that you're familiar with: Sitting in Stillness. After taking this position, remember guan, smile, and close your eyes. Then unify your mind by simply focusing on breathing deeply, noticing your abdomen going out and in as you inhale and exhale. After ten repetitions, shift your focus to the breath entering and leaving your nostrils. Don't focus on your abdomen. After ten repetitions, keep your focus on your breathing, open your eyes, and welcome the present.

After opening your eyes, try to practice Heart and Mind Fasting for five minutes. Even though your senses may be bombarded, see if you can keep your encounter with your world based in qi, or breath. See what you see, hear what you hear, and so on, but do it based in your breath. Don't let your senses or thoughts take over, control, fragment, or distract you. Don't let them disrupt your breath-based focus. If you find yourself being pulled by your senses or thoughts, don't make any judgments about this or dwell on it; just return your attention to your breath.

Afterward, reflect upon what happened when you practiced Heart and Mind Fasting. When you first opened your eyes, what did you notice? How did you feel? During the five minutes after you opened your eyes, what happened? What did you notice? Did you have any desires or thoughts? Did you get any sense of the emptiness associated with Heart and Mind Fasting? Were you fully engaged in an integrated present, with no sense of a separate and distinct self? In other words, was your mind still and empty of any thoughts and desires, including thoughts and desires about yourself? Did you feel as if you were part of the world around you? Or was your mind agitated and galloping about with thoughts and desires, especially about yourself? Did you feel fragmented, distinct, or separated from the world around you? You may wish to write about this in your journal.

Sitting in Oblivion or Forgetfulness

Whereas Heart and Mind Fasting is concerned with the elimination of excessive, stress-producing desires and selfishness and the sense of an absolute self associated with and generated by them, Sitting in Oblivion or Forgetfulness is concerned with the elimination of absolute distinctions, concepts, values, and judgments and the sense of self associated with and generated by them. Both are concerned with stilling the mind and body and emptying them of barriers and restrictions. Therefore, both help eliminate chronic stress and promote health and well-being.

The primary focus of Sitting in Oblivion or Forgetfulness is immediacy, as this practice involves being completely absorbed in the here and now (Kohn 2010b). This practice is quite spiritual in nature, culminating in the experiential realization that we are the same as Tao. This is achieved through a process in which all knowledge, sensations, forms, distinctions, concepts, values, judgments, and partiality and the sense of a separate self are forgotten (Guo 1974). They are forgotten in the same sense that fish are oblivious to the water they swim in, we are oblivious to the air we breathe, we are oblivious to the comfortable shoes we are wearing, and so on.

In this practice, there is no inner awareness of a distinct, separate body, or outer awareness of a distinct, separate world. Everything is simply forgotten. There is just the vastness where the continual and unobstructed process of change becomes form. There are no distinctions or judgments. All things are the same.

Of the various types of meditation, Sitting in Oblivion or Forgetfulness has the greatest focus on proper body alignment and posture, although proper alignment is clearly important in the other types of meditation. Proper sitting may be compared to a growing plant. The top of the plant reaches upward (yang) toward the sun, while its roots move downward (yin) to stabilize itself in the ground. This stretches the stem of the plant, allows it to be flexible, and opens it up to nourishment from the sky and the earth (Guo 1974; Karlgren 1975).

Using the plant as an example, proper sitting gently stretches and straightens the spine as the head smoothly moves upward and the lower half of the body sinks and roots downward. As a result, the body is naturally aligned and centered.

Once the body is properly aligned, the practice is simply to sit quietly, let go of any concerns, and not dwell on or think about anything. When you don't dwell on or think about anything, you won't be affected by anything. Chronic stress is eliminated. You will be aligned, rooted, and centered. Being centered, you will naturally become still and empty and merge with Tao.

Practice   Sitting in Oblivion or Forgetfulness

Once again, take the posture Sitting in Stillness. Gaze forward with your eyes gently and partially shut. Focus your attention on your abdomen expanding and contracting as you inhale and exhale. Continue to focus on your abdomen while inhaling and exhaling until you feel a sense of calmness. At this point, don't focus on anything. Without any thoughts, judgments, or distinctions, just experience the present.

If you find yourself getting distracted, don't make any judgments. Simply refocus on your breathing until you once again feel calm. Initially, practice this meditation for about ten minutes.

Upon finishing this meditation, note how you feel. Is your mind still and empty of thoughts and judgments? Were you able to embrace the present during the process? Is your sense of self more fluid and less rigid or fixed? Do you feel more integrated with the world around you? Do you have any sense of being stressed? You may wish to write about this in your journal, Again, the key is consistent and regular practice. It takes time to develop.

Interlude

I hope you practiced all the techniques described in the first part of this chapter, and that your exploration of these practices gave you a deeper, fuller experience and understanding of the Taoist meditative core and its benefits. I also hope it gave you a more complete appreciation of the qigong practices you've learned throughout this book. No matter what you do, a still and empty mind is fundamental if your interactions are to be free from chronic stress.

Qigong

We will now turn our attention to the eighth posture in the Baduanjin and Yijinjing sequences. These are the last moving postures in these sequences. Both focus on the arms and legs.

Upon finishing each sequence with the new movements, reflect upon your experiences while performing it. What were your body and mind telling you about yourself? Take some time to write in your journal about what you experienced while performing these movements.

Practice   Posture 8 of the Baduanjin Sequence: Touching Your Toes

Continue on from the previous posture, Rowing a Boat, where you are sitting up straight with your legs extended out in front of you, toes pointing up, and hands resting in your lap. Begin by taking a deep breath and slowly letting it out. Take another deep breath and scoop your hands inward, palms facing up and middle fingers slightly touching. Pause in front of your belly button. Then, as you slowly exhale, slowly raise your hands, palms still facing up and middle fingers touching, keeping your elbows down. Raise your hands until they're in line with the base of your neck. At this point, rotate your hands inward, downward, outward, and upward until your palms are facing up. Continue the motion, pushing your palms upward until your arms are extended, but without locking your elbows. Visualize your palms pushing against a ceiling. Then, still exhaling slowly, bend forward at your waist, keeping your back straight and rotating your hands outward so that your fingers point toward and are in line with your toes. Gently touch your toes with your fingers. If you can't reach your toes, that's okay. Just let your fingers touch your ankles, shins, or knees. Pause for a moment.

Slowly take a deep breath, and then slowly let it out. Then let your hands slide down the sides of your feet or legs until they are on the floor next to your legs. While slowly inhaling, slowly sit back up, focusing on and using your abdomen and letting your palms slide along the outside of your legs until you return to the starting position.

The entire process of extending your arms overhead, bending forward, and returning to the starting position constitutes one repetition. Repeat eight more times, for a total of nine repetitions. After the last repetition, pull your legs back and return to the posture Sitting in Stillness. Reflect upon what you feel.

This posture stretches the backs of the legs and the back and arms. It also enhances the circulation of qi and blood throughout the body. In addition, it cultivates attention and concentration and, as a result, stills and empties the mind, which helps eliminate chronic stress.

Practice Posture 8 of the Yijinjing Sequence: The Body Sinking and Rising

From the Wuji Standing posture, which you returned to after Nine Ghosts Pulling a Saber, take a deep breath through your nose. At the same time, scoop your hands inward, palms facing up and middle fingers slightly touching, and slowly raise your hands up, palms still facing up and middle fingers touching, keeping your elbows down. Raise your hands until they're in line with the middle of your chest. At this point, rotate your hands inward and then downward until your palms are facing the ground.

Shift your weight to your right foot and step out to the side with your left foot so that your feet are shoulder-width apart (a little wider is okay). At the same time, gently pull your hands out to the sides, keeping your hands at chest level and your palms facing down. At this point, begin to slowly exhale through your nose and push your palms down to waist level as you slowly bend your legs and lower your rear end so that your body sinks. Keep your back straight. You are essentially performing a squat. Visualize each of your palms pushing down on a table. Pause for a moment.

Slowly take a deep breath through your nose. Then, as you begin to slowly exhale through your mouth, slowly straighten your legs. At the same time, rotate your palms inward and upward, curling your hands into fists with your palms facing up, and slowly pull them up to chest level. Visualize that each fist is holding a handle connected to a pulley system that's attached to a heavy weight. When you're straightening your legs and pulling your fists up, visualize yourself moving a heavy weight upward. Pause. Then slowly inhale through your nose and sink down to the squatting position with both of your hands pushing down on a table.

The sequence from the squatting position to the upright position and back to squatting again constitutes one repetition. Repeat four more times, for a total of five repetitions. After the last repetition, return to the Wuji Standing posture.

This posture stretches and strengthens the legs, arms, abdomen, and waist. It also enhances the flow of qi in the lower dantian. The use of visualization strengthens attention and concentration and also assists in stilling and emptying the mind, which is beneficial for eliminating chronic stress.

Conclusion

This chapter focused on the foundation of the nonspecific, nonintentional, and body-grounded Taoist approach to stilling and emptying the mind and managing or eliminating chronic stress: the Taoist meditative core. Practicing all four elements of the meditative core regularly—Breathing from Your Heels, Mind Like a Mirror, Heart and Mind Fasting, and Sitting in Oblivion or Forgetfulness—will give you a better understanding of the Taoist path and how it harmonizes yin and yang approaches to eliminating chronic stress. The next chapter, which is the last chapter in the book, explores how this harmonization is manifested in the Taoist role model: the authentic person.

Chapter 10

The Authentic Person

From ancient times until the present, the *zhenren*, or authentic person, has been the role model for practitioners of Taoism. The earliest description of the zhenren appears in the *Zhuangzi* (Guo 1974), written over 2,200 years ago. The authentic person is described as obtaining stress-free, restful, and sufficient sleep. When she is awake, she isn't chronically stressed. She eats moderately. Her mind is still and empty of agitation. She doesn't have absolute thoughts, beliefs, or judgments, or other forms of negative thinking. Her mind, body, and behavior are all in harmony with the continual process of change and transformation. She doesn't interfere with herself, others, or the world around her. She doesn't get entangled in the activities of the world. She doesn't fear death or relish life. Her life is quite simple. She is happy, carefree, and at peace. She is integrated with Tao.

In the *Zhuangzi*, the authentic person, who is clearly free from chronic stress, is compared to the person who is chronically stressed. The breath is key to this distinction. The authentic person is described as breathing very deeply, from her heels, whereas the chronically-stressed person is described as breathing very shallowly, from his throat. His breathing is restricted, giving rise to a retching sound when he talks. This compromised breathing is linked to an agitated mind and body, unresolved desires, and a long-standing pattern of being uncentered, unrooted, unstable, and superficial.

In what is believed to be the earliest Chinese medical text, the *Neijing*, the authentic person of ancient times is described as reaching the highest state of health and well-being and therefore having the greatest longevity. The fundamental reason for his good health, well-being, and freedom from chronic stress was that he understood and was guided, cognitively, physically, and interpersonally, by the interrelated, continually changing and transforming process of yin and yang. He realized that there are no absolutes, cognitively or physically, because everything is subject to the continual process of change and transformation. He focused on the positive and life affirming, rather than the negative or life denying. He turned his attention to vitality, not lethargy; facilitating, not impeding; and enjoying, not disliking. He also practiced moderation, balancing between excessive and deficient in all of his behavior—cognitive, physical, and interpersonal. Therefore, he was in harmony with himself and the world around him.

The authentic person's daily life was consistent and regular. He did not labor excessively. He was concerned with getting restful and adequate sleep, eating and drinking in moderation, stretching, and exercising in the form of brisk walking. He also practiced *yangsheng*, or cultivating life, by practicing correct breathing, inhaling and exhaling qi and jing (life essence) while standing alone (Standing like a Tree or Stake in the Ground), and observing, guarding, and embracing his spirit (shen) and thus uniting it with his body. Today, we know yangsheng as qigong.

The Three Taoist Treasures

I briefly mentioned the concepts jing and shen earlier in this book. Now I'd like to take a closer look. In Taoism, the human being consists of three basic interrelated components, or treasures: qi, jing, and shen. Reintegrating these three treasures is a fundamental spiritual goal for the authentic person, and a prerequisite for this reintegration is eliminating chronic stress.

As noted earlier in the book, qi is vital energy and breath. It takes on various shapes, configurations, and qualities through the workings of yin and yang. It circulates throughout the universe and throughout our bodies. It is the basic building block of all things organic, where it combines with jing, and inorganic. We maintain our lives through the qi we receive via breathing, eating, and drinking. Jing is the life essence or life force. It is coarse, condensed, and concrete qi. Our lives are also maintained through the jing we receive via breathing, eating, and drinking. Shen is consciousness and spirit. It is fine, thin, and intangible qi.

Psychologically, qi is associated with our emotions, jing is associated with our desires, and shen is associated with our cognitive activity, such as attention, concentration, beliefs, judgments, thoughts, and thinking. All three treasures are intertwined and linked to all of our behaviors. Excessive or deficient emotions drain qi. Excessive or deficient desires drain jing. Excessive or deficient cognitive activity drains shen. The draining of qi, jing, or shen leads to an agitated mind and body, resulting in chronic stress. This underlies Taoism's focus on the necessity of moderation in all aspects of our lives.

For the authentic person, a holistic lifestyle of moderation is created by eliminating chronic stress and maintaining a harmonious relationship between jing, qi, and shen. What and how much we eat, what and how much we drink, how much and how well we sleep, whether and how much we exercise and meditate, the simplicity of our lives, whether our desires are excessive or deficient, how we interact with others and the world, and how we think, feel, and behave—all of these things have a direct impact on our jing, qi, and shen; on being centered, rooted, and stabilized; and on maintaining a harmonious relationship between mind, body, and environment.

The Authentic Person and the Art of Calculation

The authentic person is sensitive to, responsive to, and integrated with the world around her and all that entails, and to her own body and mind. This isn't due to some magical potion or sudden epiphany. It is due to the application of a strategy that is flexible, noncontrived, and nonscheming, as noted in both the *Zhuangzi* (Guo 1974) and *Neijing* (2007). This allows the authentic person to be in harmony within herself and with the world. This strategy of self-monitoring provides guidance and requires discipline, attention, concentration, effort, and ongoing consistent practice.

One description of this strategy is found in the ancient text known as the *Bingfa*. Originally developed as a manual on warfare, this Taoist-influenced text is still used in many Asian countries for guidance on how to manage business affairs. To a certain degree, you have been learning to use the same guidelines throughout this book, applying them to addressing chronic stress.

The five steps in this pattern of guidance, based on chapter 4 of the *Bingfa*, are utilized for assessing, analyzing, and evaluating chronic stress and coming up with solutions to the underlying problems creating the stress (Sunzi 2012). Once the problem has been identified, the following five steps are applied:

1. Gathering information from various contexts

2. Measuring the information

3. Analyzing the information and generating solutions

4. Evaluating the analysis

5. Making a decision, acting on it, and monitoring the results

In order to make the application of these five steps concrete, I'll apply them to Martha's situation. As you may recall from the story in chapter 7, Martha had a problem with excessive texting.

1. Gathering Information from Various Contexts

The focus of the first step is on gathering information about what occurred and where. In Martha's case, the problems are poor sleep, poor nutrition, being late for work, poor work performance, physical pain, poor attention and concentration on activities other than texting, being physically and psychologically drained, and, ultimately, a car accident. The numerous contexts where her problems occurred include at home, at work, and while driving down the street.

2. Measuring the Information

Given the information gathered in the first step, the focus of the second step is on calculating how often, how long, and when the problematic behaviors occur. This step would be applied to all the identified problems. For example, Martha has been noticing pain in her wrist, fingers, thumb, shoulder, and neck. It is occurring on a daily basis, lasts for about an hour, and appears to happen every time she texts.

3. Analyzing the Information and Generating Solutions

Given the problem and its frequency, duration, and link to a specific behavior, the next step is to ask what can be done with the information. What does the information tell us about the cause of the problem? Can the cause be connected to other identified problems? In Martha's case, the cause of her physical pain seems quite obvious: she's spending too much time texting. She appears to have a repetitive use injury. Her excessive texting can also be easily linked to her other identified problems, such as lack of sleep, poor eating habits, and lack of energy. In other words, Martha's excessive texting has resulted in her being chronically stressed physically, psychologically, interpersonally, and occupationally.

Given that excessive texting has been identified as the cause of Martha's pain, and given that texting is also clearly linked to Martha's other identified problems, the immediate solution is to stop texting or at least significantly reduce how much time she spends texting. In addition, given her chronic stress, she needs to take a proactive approach to generating solutions. For starters, she might consider exercising, meditating, and changing her eating habits.

4. Evaluating the Analysis

The potential solutions must be evaluated. We need to consider what value we place on each potential solution and the benefits each might confer. We also need to consider the consequences of not implementing each solution. In Martha's case, one potential solution is eliminating or at least reducing her texting. If she doesn't implement this solution, her pain will probably get worse, she many lose her job, and she will remain chronically stressed. What are the consequences of implementing this solution? In all likelihood, both her pain and her chronic stress will be reduced. It's also important to consider whether proposed solutions may have negative consequences. In Martha's case, decreasing her texting time may lead to problems with her friends. If such problems arise, they can be addressed using this same five-step process.

5. Making a Decision, Acting on It, and Monitoring the Results

Given the evaluation and the weight of the evidence, the next step is to choose a solution and implement it. Given Martha's obsession with texting, she may opt to reduce her texting, rather than completely eliminating it. It's also necessary to monitor the effectiveness of all solutions. Martha needs to monitor how effective her solution is in decreasing her pain and easing or eliminating her chronic stress. The same five-step process should be applied to monitoring the results.

The Authentic Person and Visualization

The *Neijing*'s description of the authentic person, who integrates qi, jing, and shen, is consistent with a later Taoist practice known as internal alchemy. A fundamental goal of internal alchemy is the integration of qi, jing, and shen to become a zhenren, or authentic person. One method used to achieve this is visualization.

I've discussed visualization in the context of both Breathing from Your Heels and Mind Like a Mirror. However, visualization is a type of meditation in its own right. In fact, it appears to be the most frequently practiced type of meditation across Taoist history (Kohn 2008b). Visualization is a creative, actively directed process that is used, like all types of meditation, to alter how practitioners think, feel, and behave, and to center and root them, thus eliminating chronic stress. It is a fundamental practice for the authentic person.

In many cases, visualization is used to generate, cultivate, refine, and guide the flow of qi throughout the body. As such, it trains attention and concentration while stilling and emptying the mind and body of agitation. In the Taoist view, this process can be used to heal both body and mind and eliminate stress by visualizing meridians or channels running through the body, various organs, different parts of the body, and so on. Taoists also use it as a spiritual practice that cultivates connection and merging with the earth and sky, various deities that inhabit both the external world and the internal world of the person, and Tao itself.

Practice   The Microcosmic Orbit Visualization

The Microcosmic Orbit Visualization is a practice that activates the flow of qi through the two main qi reservoirs in the body: the *ren mai* (yin) and the *du mai* (yang). The du mai, or governing channel, runs from the *huiyin* point, which is between your genitals and anus, up your back along your spine and over the top of your head, and ends at the roof of your mouth just behind your front teeth. The ren mai, or conception channel, begins at the root of your tongue and runs down the front centerline of your body, along your throat, solar plexus, and belly button, and past your genitals to the huiyin point.

The Microcosmic Orbit visualization can be practiced sitting (on the ground or in a chair) or standing. Maintain the proper posture you've learned in this book, with your head being gently pulled up, your shoulders relaxed and down, and your back straight but not rigid, as in the Sitting in Stillness and Wuji Standing postures. Be sure to smile and apply guan throughout this practice.

Gently touch the tip of your tongue to the roof of your mouth just behind your front teeth. This connects the ren mai and du mai channels and makes a complete circuit in your body. Take a deep, slow breath through your nose, allowing your abdomen to expand, and then slowly exhale through your nose, allowing your abdomen to contract. Repeat this two more times.

Next, focus on the huiyin point, between your genitals and anus, and as you begin to slowly inhale through your nose, visualize your breath slowly ascending from this point through a tube, about the

149

width of a finger, that travels up the middle of your back and over the top of your head and comes to rest where your tongue is touching the roof of your mouth.

As you slowly exhale through your nose, visualize your breath descending from the tip of your tongue through a tube, again about the width of a finger, that travels through your tongue, down the center line of the front of your body through your sternum, solar plexus, belly button, and pelvis, and ends at the huiyin point.

One ascending of the breath (yang) and one descending of the breath (yin) constitutes one cycle of the microcosmic orbit. When your breath reaches the *huiyin* point, begin again. Repeat for twenty-five cycles. Then take notice of what you feel. Do you feel more rooted and centered? Does your mind feel still and empty? Are you less stressed? Did you get any sense of a tingling, a fullness, warmth, pulsating, or flow along the pathway of the microcosmic orbit? All of these sensations are indicative of qi circulating through your body. The more you practice, the stronger the sensations will be. If you don't feel anything initially, that's okay. For most people it takes time to cultivate the flow of qi. Remember, the key is consistent and regular practice.

The Authentic Person and Smiling

In June of 2009, I attended and presented a paper at a conference on Taoism on Wudang Mountain, in Hubei Province in China. Wudang Mountain is a very famous in Taoism and is associated with internal martial arts and qigong. According to legend, taijiquan was invented on Wudang Mountain by Zhang Sanfeng, believed to be a zhonren and practitioner of Quanzhan (Complete Reality) Taoism during the Yuan (1271-1367) and Ming (1368-1644) dynasties..

While attending the conference, I met up with David Wei, a former student of mine at Chaminade University. David had been living on Wudang Mountain since 2006, training in Taoist martial arts, qigong, and meditation. He is a formal disciple of Master Yuan Xiu Gang. I also met up with Penghong Teh, a businessman from Malaysia whom I'd met at a previous conference on Taoism in China. One afternoon David took Penghong and me on a tour of the mountain. After visiting some of the more well-known sites, he took us off the beaten track to meet with a Taoist hermit monk who lived in a cave on the side of the mountain. As we approached his cave, we could see the monk in his blue gown and Taoist hat. Even though we were still some distance from his cave, his smile radiated through the forest. As we got closer, we all clearly felt his inner power. Were we seeing and feeling an authentic person?

David, who knew the monk fairly well, went ahead to talk with him. When we reached the monk, his smile was overwhelming. After David introduced us, the monk gave David three persimmons. We each ate one of the fruits. As David munched on his persimmon, he said the monk had been expecting us. Earlier, the monk had received a visitor who gave him the three persimmons and told him that he would soon have three visitors and should give the fruits to them. Needless to say, this was a jaw-dropping experience. The monk looked at us with his penetrating smile and just laughed. His smile and laughter were quite contagious. The feeling of interacting with each other and eating fruit in a forest next to a cave on the side of a mountain while in the presence of the overwhelming smile of this Taoist monk was indescribable. The closest I can come is to say I felt no stress and had a profound sense of oneness.

Clearly, a spontaneous smile is a fundamental aspect of the authentic person. It is also quite beneficial both physically and psychologically, as demonstrated by recent research (Kraft and Pressman 2012).

The Authentic Person and Laughter

One of the defining characteristics of the authentic person is that he doesn't take himself too seriously. He is able to laugh at himself, laugh with others, and laugh at the absurdities in the world around him (Guo 1974). This is one of the ways he protects himself from chronic stress and integrates with others and the world around him. Recent research appears to support the observation that laughter helps reduce stress (Mayo Clinic Staff 2010; Berk, Tan, and Berk 2008).

The authentic person's laughter, which begins with a smile, further removes problematic, stress-producing entanglements, desires, thoughts, beliefs, judgments, and behaviors as it permeates everything. It is in the realm of genuine smiling and laughter that the authentic person sees and experiences others of like mind and like heart. This is where he finds his true friends and mate.

When you are truly smiling or laughing, your mind is still and empty. There is no negativity. Try it right now: smile—not a forced, fake smile, but an authentic one. How do you feel? As you smile, try to think negatively. You cannot truly smile when negative thoughts are present. If a negative thought pops in, either you are no longer smiling or your smile isn't authentic.

The next time you laugh (which should be a daily occurrence), notice how you feel and what occurs in your body and mind. When we laugh authentically, we are free of negativity and stress.

Authentic smiling and laughing are fundamental aspects of the Taoist path to removing chronic stress. Smiling and laughter are natural and neither excessive nor deficient, and as such, they harmonize mind and body and put us in harmony with our environment.

Even though consistently practicing both the mental and physical components of the Taoist path to the removal of chronic stress is necessary and of the utmost importance, to fully eliminate chronic stress from your life and allow your yin and yang to be in harmony, you need to smile and laugh. It simply won't work otherwise!

The Authentic Person and Proper Body Alignment

In June of 2007, I was studying baguazhang (a martial art that is focused on moving in circles), taijiquan, and qigong at Beijing Sports University in Beijing, China. One of the workshops I attended was conducted by a master of qigong and Wu-style taijiquan. He emphasized the importance of correct posture and how correct posture, correct breathing, and a peaceful mind are all interrelated in the practice of taijiquan, qigong, and meditation in general.

The master taught us a technique fundamental to all Chinese martial arts and qigong: Zhan Zhuang, or Standing Like a Tree or Stake in the Ground, which you should be familiar with by now. He observed each of the participants individually and made corrections. He came up to me and said my breathing was too noisy because my body wasn't in the proper alignment. He then proceeded to align my posture by simply touching and gently pushing a few parts of my body with one finger. His subtle corrections centered me, quieted my breath, stilled my mind, and gave me the sensation of being suspended from above, much like a puppet being pulled up by a string on its head. The overall result was a feeling of being naturally and deeply relaxed.

Whether we are sitting, standing, or moving, if our bodies aren't in the proper posture, aligned and rooted, we won't be stable or centered. If we aren't centered, the flow of qi will be compromised and our minds can't be still. The authentic person's body is properly aligned.

The Authentic Person, Community, and Family

While there are Taoists who are hermits and live by themselves in search of spiritual awakening, most followers of Taoism belong to religious communities. Some of these individuals practice celibacy (monastics in Quanzhen Taoism), while others are married and have families (Tianshi Taoism).

For the authentic person, interacting with others is a natural process. It is with others that we share our experiences, thoughts, beliefs, and emotions. With others we cry, smile, and laugh. We are all part of the same continually changing process called Tao. It is with others that we find support, friendship, family, and love. With others, we can grow. We need to see and experience our thinking, beliefs, feelings, and behavior in relation to other people. We are not separate. While other people may contribute to our chronic stress, it is also other people who assist us in eliminating it. For the authentic person, the journey of life must be shared. It is through sharing, while rooted and centered with an empty and still mind, that we leave chronic stress behind.

Interlude

The first part of this chapter examined the Taoist role model of the authentic person, or zhenren, who is the epitome of good health, well-being, and freedom from chronic stress. The authentic person is sensitive and responsive to body, mind, and environment—qualities we can develop through the physical practice of qigong.

Qigong

In this final section on qigong, you'll learn the closing postures for the two sequences of eight movements you've learned: Baduanjin and Yijinjing. In addition, you'll learn the opening movement for the Yang style of taijiquan. Although taijiquan was initially developed as a form of self-defense, it has evolved over time to have the same functions for health and well-being as various forms of qigong. Remember, for any qigong and taijiquan postures to be effective in removing and eliminating chronic stress, you must practice them on a regular and consistent basis, applying guan and smiling. And if you find yourself suddenly laughing as you work through the postures, great!

Upon finishing each sequence, with all eight postures plus the closing posture, reflect upon your experiences while performing it. What were your body and mind telling you about yourself? Take some time to write in your journal about what you experienced while performing these movements.

Practice   The Closing Posture of the Baduanjin Sequence

The closing posture of the Baduanjin sequence is essentially the same as the basic Sitting in Stillness posture, with two exceptions. The first is how you hold your hands. From the posture Sitting in Stillness, which you returned to after the posture Touching Your Toes, make a ring with the thumb and first finger of your left hand, touching the tips together. Push the thumb of your right hand through the ring and wrap the fingers of your left hand around your thumb. Then wrap the fingers of your right hand around the fingers of your left hand. Place your hands on your abdomen with the inside of both wrists touching your abdomen just below your belly button. Your elbows should be down. This configuration is known as the joining of yin and yang or, more commonly, the *taiji* diagram.

The second difference is that, once in this position, you practice Sitting in Oblivion or Forgetfulness. Look forward with your eyes gently and partially closed. Focus your attention on your abdomen expanding and contracting as you inhale and exhale until you feel a sense of calmness. Then don't focus on anything. Simply breathe naturally, without any thoughts, judgments, or distinctions, and experience the present. Once you feel a sense of calmness, practice Sitting in Oblivion or Forgetfulness for five minutes. Remember to smile. If you find yourself getting distracted, refocus on your breathing until you feel calm again.

Upon finishing this posture, note what you feel. Is your stress gone, at least for the moment? Then take a deep breath and slowly let it out. Push your legs out in front of you and gently stretch them. Release your hands from the taiji diagram configuration and gently shake your hands and arms. When you feel ready, stand up and walk away.

Practice   The Closing Posture of the Yijinjing Sequence

From the Wuji Standing posture, which you returned to after the posture The Body Sinking and Rising, take a slow, deep breath and let your arms rise up to the sides until they're level with your shoulders, with your palms facing down and your fingers extending out to the sides. Rotate your hands so your little fingers move downward and your thumbs move upward until your palms face upward. Continue to raise your arms, keeping them extended but not locking your elbows, until your hands come together above your head with the tips of your fingers and thumbs gently touching and pointing upward. Complete your inhalation as your hands come together. You should have a sensation that your chest, back, and abdomen are being stretched. You should also feel the backs of your legs, especially your calves, being stretched. Hold this position for about thirty seconds, breathing naturally.

Then, while slowly exhaling, leave your hands together with fingers and thumbs pointing upward and slowly lower your arms in front of you until your hands are in line with the middle of your chest, approximately six to twelve inches in front of your sternum. Your shoulders and elbows should be down. Complete your exhalation as your hands, shoulders, and elbows come to rest.

Finally, breathing naturally and not focusing on anything in particular, hold the posture for five minutes. Remember to smile. If you find yourself getting distracted, direct your attention to your breathing until you feel centered and focused. After five minutes, let your arms gently lower to your sides. Note what you feel. Is your chronic stress gone, at least for the time being, upon finishing the sequence?

Practice   The Opening Posture of the Yang Style of Taijiquan

Start from the Wuji Standing posture, with your eyes open and looking forward. Take a slow, deep breath, shift your weight to your right leg, and step out to the side with your left foot so that your feet are about shoulder-width apart and your weight is evenly distributed. Slowly exhale. Your knees should be slightly bent and in line with your toes, not extending past your toes. Let your arms hang down alongside your body, with your palms facing the rear.

As you slowly inhale once again, very slowly and gently let your arms rise and arc up to the front until they're level with and in line with your shoulders. Your arms should extend forward, your elbows shouldn't be locked, and your palms should face down. Complete your inhalation as your arms reach the level of your shoulders. There should be no tension anywhere in your body. Without moving your head, watch your hands as they rise up.

Once your arms reach the level of your shoulders and your inhalation is complete, slowly exhale and allow your arms to gently sink down to your sides, following the path by which they arose. Without moving your head, watch your hands as they sink down.

Raising and lowering your arms once constitutes one repetition. Leaving your feet in the same position, repeat nine more times, for a total of ten repetitions. At the completion of the tenth repetition, shift your weight to your right leg and return your left foot to its original position. Note what you feel. Do you feel centered, rooted, and stable? Is your mind still and empty? Do you have sensations of qi flowing, such as your arms or hands feeling heavy, feeling light, tingling, pulsating, or feeling like a hose full of water?

As you perform this posture, try to focus on using your legs, abdomen, back, chest, and shoulders to both raise and lower your arms, but doing so without creating tension anywhere in your body. You aren't just lifting and lowering your arms. The purpose of focusing your eyes on your hands as you do the movements is to still and empty your mind of any agitation and also to activate the flow of qi. Qi follows the focus or intention of your mind. So in addition to training your attention and concentration, this posture is about gathering, refining, and circulating qi throughout your body. Take a moment to reflect on your experience: as a result of practicing this posture, what is the status of your chronic stress?

Conclusion

This chapter introduced you to the Taoist role model known as the zhenren, or authentic person. The authentic person follows the Taoist path by consistently practicing both the mental and physical components and by not taking himself too seriously. As a result, the authentic person, smiling and laughing, is in harmony with his environment and isn't chronically stressed.

Moving Forward

I hope your journey along the Taoist path toward eliminating chronic stress has been and continues to be a fulfilling and worthwhile experience. You have come a long way since you took that first step. Congratulations on staying the course.

You've learned several basic concepts and techniques that can assist you in eliminating and preventing chronic stress by calming, balancing, and simplifying your life. Utilize both the mental and physical approaches. Believe in yourself, practice moderation, and be flexible. Remember to smile and laugh on a daily basis. Incorporate guan into your life. Stay in the present. Put all of this into practice on a consistent and regular basis.

Essentially, the teachings of Taoism are about being in harmony with the continually changing process we call life and therefore being free from chronic stress. To be in harmony with life means staying within certain boundaries. Your yin and yang need to be in harmony so your qi can circulate freely.

This book guided you in seeing how excessive and deficient behaviors across many interrelated areas, such as thoughts, beliefs, judgments, desires, feelings, and actions, can lead to chronic stress. It has offered guidance in simplifying your life, reducing desires, and stilling and emptying your mind so you can free yourself from chronic stress. Having become aware of excessive and deficient behaviors, and having examined those behaviors and generated solutions, both mental and physical, you are well on your way to easing or eliminating your chronic stress.

Ultimately, the focus of this book has been on helping you return to a harmonious relationship with life and all that it entails so your journey might be free from chronic stress. I'd like to leave you with these words from chapter 42 of the *Daodejing* (Wang 1993, 169):

All things carry yin on their backside and embrace yang in the front.

Because they are centered and rooted in the empty space in between, they are in harmony as their qi swirls and circulates freely.

References

American Psychological Association (APA). 2007. *Stress in America Survey 2007.* http.apa.org/pubs/info/reports/2007-stress.doc; accessed December 12, 2011.

———. 2008. *Stress in America Survey 2008.* http.apa.org/news/press /releases/2008/10/stress-in-america.pdf; accessed December 12, 2011.

———. 2009. *Stress in America Survey 2009.* http.apa.org/news/press /releases/stress-exec-summary.pdf; accessed December 12, 2011.

———. 2010. *Stress in America Survey 2010.* http.apa.org/news/press /releases/stress/national-report.pdf; accessed December 12, 2011.

———. 2012. *Stress in America Survey 2011.* http.apa.org/news/press/ releases/stress/2011/final-2011.pdf; accessed 1/22/12.

Baike. 2007. *Taiqing Daoyin Yangsheng Jing.* http://baike.baidu.com /view/934892.htm; accessed February 27, 2013.

Benson, H. 1998. "Statement of Herbert Benson, MD, President, Mind/ Body Medical Institute," in *Mind/Body Medicine: Hearing Before a Subcommittee of the Committee on Appropriations United States Senate One Hundred Fifth Congress Second Session. Special Hearing.* Washington, DC: Government Printing Office.

Berk, L. S., S. A. Tan, and D. Berk. 2008. "Cortisol and Catecholamine Stress Hormone Decrease Is Associated with the Behavior of

Perceptual Anticipation of Mirthful Laughter." *FASEB Journal* 22:946.11.

Bouchez, C. 2011. "Can Stress Cause Weight Gain? How to Keep the World's Woes from Weighing You Down." http://webmd.com/diet/features/can-stress-cause-weight-gain; accessed December 24, 2011.

Colbert, D. 2006. *The Seven Pillars of Health: The Natural Way to Better Health for Life*. Lake Mary, FL: Siloam.

Dallman, M. F. 2009. "Stress Induced Obesity and the Emotional Nervous System." *Trends in Endocrinology and Metabolism* 21(3):159–165.

Davis, M. D., and J. A. Hayes. 2011. "What Are the Benefits of Mindfulness? A Practice Review of Psychotherapy-Related Research." *Psychotherapy* 48(2):198–208.

Guo, Q. F. 1974. *Zhuangzi Jishi*. Taipei: Chung Hwa. www.hudong.com/wiki/%E6%9D%A8%E6%BE%84%E7%94%AB; accessed April 1, 2012.

Guanzi. 2012. *Neiye*. http://homepage.ntu.edu.tw/~duhbauruei/5rso/texts/1chim/te10/49.htm; accessed February 12, 2012.

Harvard Health. 2009. "Walking: Your Steps to Health." *Harvard Men's Health Watch*, August. http://health.harvard.edu/newsletters/Harvard_Mens_Health_Watch/2009/August/Walking-Your-steps-to-health; accessed August 6, 2012.

———. 2012. "Why Stress Causes People to Overeat." *Harvard Mental Health Letter*, February. http.health.harvard.edu/newsletters/Harvard_Mental_Health_Letter/2012/February/why-stress-causes-people-to-overeat; accessed January 3, 2013.

Howes, R. 2011. "Journaling in Therapy." Blog entry. http://psychologytoday.com/blog/in-therapy/201101/journaling-in-therapy; accessed January 15, 2013.

Jahnke, R., L. Larkey, C. Rogers, J. Etnier, and F. Lin. 2010. "A Comprehensive Review of Health Benefits of Qigong and Tai Chi." *American Journal of Health Promotion* 24(6):e1–e25.

Karlgren, B. 1975. *Analytical Dictionary of Chinese and Sino-Japanese.* Taipei: Ch'eng-Wen Publishing Company.

Kohn, L. 2008a. *Chinese Healing Exercises: The Tradition of Daoyin.* Honolulu: University of Hawaii Press.

———. 2010a. *Daoist Dietetics: Food for Immortality.* Dunedin, FL: Three Pines Press.

———. 2008b. *Meditation Works in the Daoist, Buddhist, and Hindu Traditions.* Magdalena, NM: Three Pines Press.

———. 2010a. *Daoist Dietetics: Food for Immortality.* Dunedin, FL: Three Pines Press.

———. 2010b. *Sitting in Oblivion: The Heart of Daoist Meditation.* Dunedin, FL: Three Pines Press.

———. 2012. *A Sourcebook in Chinese Longevity.* St. Petersburg, FL: Three Pines Press.

Kraft, T. L., and S. D. Pressman. 2012. "Grin and Bear It: The Influence of Manipulated Facial Expressions on the Stress Response." *Psychological Science* 23(11):1372–1378.

Mayo Clinic Staff. 2010. "Stress Release from Laughter? Yes, No Joke." http://mayoclinic.com/health/stress-relief/SR00034; accessed January 14, 2013.

McEwen, B., with E. N. Lasley. 2002. *The End of Stress as We Know It.* Washington, DC: Joseph Henry Press.

Miller, D. 1993. "The Origins of Pa Kua Chang: Part 3." *Pa Kua Chang Journal* 3(4):25–29.

Neijing. 2007. *Huangdi Neijing.* www.chinapage.com/medicine/hw2.htm; accessed April 12, 2007.

Ratey, J. J. 2008. *Spark: The Revolutionary New Science of Exercise and the Brain.* New York: Little, Brown, and Company.

Regus. 2012. *From Distressed to De-stressed.* www.regus.presscentre.com /imagelibrary/downloadMedia.ashx?MediaDetailsID=44168; accessed January 19, 2013.

Robinet, I. 1993. *Taoist Meditation: The Mao-Shan Tradition of Great Purity*. Albany, NY: State University of New York.

Rogers, C., L. K. Larkey, and C. Keller. 2009. "A Review of Clinical Trials of Tai Chi and Qigong in Older Adults." *Western Journal of Nursing Research* 31(2):245–279.

Rosen, C. 2008. "The Myth of Multitasking." *New Atlantis*, Spring, 105–110. www.thenewatlantis.com/docLib/20080605_TNA20Rosen.pdf; accessed December 15, 2011.

Santee, R. G. 2007. *An Integrative Approach to Counseling: Bridging Chinese Thought, Evolutionary Theory, and Stress Management*. Thousand Oaks, CA: Sage Publications.

———. 2009. "Circle Walking: Daoism, Baguazhang, and the Relaxation Response." Paper Presented at the Fifth International Daoist Studies Conference, *The Past, Present, and Future of Daoism*, Wudangshan, Hubei, China.

———. 2010. "Sun Style Taiji Qigong: Taoist Internal Alchemy." *Qi: The Journal of Traditional Eastern Health and Fitness* 20(2):30–38.

———. 2011. "The Yijinjing." *Qi: The Journal of Traditional Eastern Health and Fitness* 21(2):34–43.

Saso, M. 1994. *A Taoist Cookbook, with Meditations from the Laozi Daode Jing*. Boston: Tuttle.

Scott, E. 2011. "Cortisol and Stress: How to Stay Healthy." http://stress.about.com/od/stresshealth/a/cortisol.htm; accessed December 14, 2011.

Segerstrom, S. C., and G. E. Miller. 2004. "Psychological Stress and the Human Immune System: A Meta-Analytic Study of 30 Years of Inquiry." *Psychological Bulletin* 130(4):601–630. www.ncbi.nlm.nih.gov/pmc/articles/PMC1361287; accessed December 14, 2011.

Sunzi. 2012. *Bing Fa*. www.360doc.com/content/09/1230/14/0_12304303.shtml; accessed December 20, 2012.

Tao Hongming. 2013. *Yangxing Yanming Lu*. www.taoist.org.cn/webfront/webfront_showList.cgi?dircode=1110201000000000000&#0022

;perPageNum=15&#0022;targetPage=Fdjxy3; accessed February 27, 2013.

Waehner, P. 2012. "Top 10 Reasons You Don't Exercise." http://exercise .about.com/cs/fittingitin/a/exerciseobstacl.htm; accessed September 10, 2012.

Walsh, R., and S. L. Shapiro. 2006. "The Meeting of Meditative Disciplines and Western Psychology." *American Psychologist* 61(3):227–239.

Wang, K. 1993. *Lao Zi Dao De Jing Heshang Gong Zhang Zhu.* Beijing: Zhong Hua Shu Ju.

Wayne, P. M., and M. L. Fuerst. 2013. *The Harvard Medical School Guide to Tai Chi: 12 Weeks to a Healthy Body, Strong Heart & Sharp Mind.* Boston: Shambhala.

WebMD. 2011. "The Effects of Stress on Your Body." http://webmd.com /balance/guide/effects-of-stress-on-your-body; accessed December 12, 2011.

Yang, J. L. 1972. *Zhuangzi Jijie, Liezi Zhu.* Taipei: Shi Jie Shu Ju.

Robert G. Santee, PhD, is a nationally certified counselor. He is also dean of behavioral sciences, director of the masters of science program in counseling psychology, and full professor of psychology at Chaminade University in Honolulu, HI. He is the author of *An Integrative Approach to Counseling,* and has presented at international conferences on Taoism in China and California, and at the 119th Annual Convention of the American Psychological Association in Washington, DC. Santee is certified as a Wushu (martial arts, qigong) coach (jiaolian) in Fujian Province, China, and is a senior instructor (Taijiquan and qigong) for the Xiaxing Martial Arts Association in Honolulu, HI.

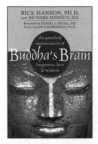